Franklin before the Privy Council, White Hall Chapel

London, 1774

Benjamin Franklin

APPLEWOOD BOOKS
Bedford, Massachusetts

Franklin before the Privy Council, White Hall Chapel
was originally published in
1860

9781429017442

★ AMERICAN REVOLUTIONARY WAR ★
SERIES

Thank you for purchasing an Applewood book. Applewood reprints America's lively classics—books from the past that are still of interest to modern readers. This facsimile was printed using many new technologies together to bring our tradition-bound mission to you. Applewood's facsimile edition of this work may include library stamps, scribbles, and margin notes as they exist in the original book. These interesting historical artifacts celebrate the place the book was read or the person who read the book. In addition to these artifacts, the work may have additional errors that were either in the original, in the digital scans, or introduced as we prepared the book for printing. If you believe the work has such errors, please let us know by writing to us at the address below.

For a free copy of our current print catalog featuring our bestselling books, write to:

APPLEWOOD BOOKS
P.O. Box 365
Bedford, MA 01730

For more complete listings, visit us on the web at:
awb.com

Prepared for publishing by HP

FRANKLIN

BEFORE THE PRIVY COUNCIL,

WHITE HALL CHAPEL, LONDON, 1774,

ON BEHALF OF THE

PROVINCE OF MASSACHUSETTS,

TO ADVOCATE THE REMOVAL OF HUTCHINSON AND OLIVER.

PHILADELPHIA:
PUBLISHED BY JOHN M. BUTLER,
242 CHESTNUT STREET.
1860.

Entered according to the Act of Congress, in the year 1859 by
JOHN M. BUTLER,
In the Clerk's Office of the District Court for the Eastern District of Pennsylvania.

STEREOTYPED BY
JESPER HARDING & SON,
INQUIRER BUILDING, SOUTH THIRD STREET, PHILADELPHIA.

INTRODUCTION.

FRANKLIN BEFORE THE LORDS IN COUNCIL

IN RELATION TO THE HUTCHINSON AND OLIVER CORRESPONDENCE.

IN Bancroft's history of the United States we have a graphic description of this striking scene, arising from one of the most important of Franklin's official transactions with his country; and which greatly accelerated the course of events resulting in the independence of the Colonies.

In 1773, Franklin was residing in London as commissioner for the Colonies of Massachusetts and Pennsylvania, and also of New Jersey and Georgia; coming to the knowledge of certain letters written by Governor Hutchinson and Lieutenant Governor Oliver, of the province of Massachusetts, to persons in power and office in England, calling for suppressive measures, and advising action detrimental to the interest of the colonies; and subsequently obtaining possession of the letters, he transmitted copies of them to the Speaker of the Assembly of Massachusetts; at the same time calling attention to the insidious character of the documents, and the unfaithful character of their public officers. The perusal of these letters excited the greatest indignation. The House of Representatives respectfully petitioned his Majesty for the removal of the Governor and Lieutenant Governor; charging them with betraying their trust, and the people they governed; and with giving private, partial, and false information to those in power. They also declared them enemies to the colonies, and prayed for their speedy removal from office.

It was upon this question that Franklin came before the Council, assisted by John Dunning and John Lee, to advocate the removal of Hutchinson and Oliver. It was the general opinion in America, that

Hutchinson ought to be superseded. Wedderburn, the Solicitor General, who appeared in behalf of Hutchinson and Oliver, changed the issue as if Franklin were on trial; and in a speech, replete with falsehood and invective, charged him with the vilest conduct in obtaining and using the letters. This infamous speech was received with cheers and laughter by the Lords in council, who regarded it as a triumph over the venerable Franklin and the cause he advocated. It is the narrative of this extraordinary scene that forms the chapter in Bancroft's history, entitled "The King in Council insults the great American Plebeian."

An event having so direct an influence on the future of the country, and which may be said to have fully awakened the spirit of liberty, cannot fail to be appreciated at the present time. In the splendid engraving of this subject which this volume accompanies, the historical importance and truthfulness of the event, together with the intrinsic qualities of the work,—having been produced by a combination of talent never before employed on any similar publication,—must commend it as a work of great value to the American public.

This magnificent picture is one of the largest ever published in the country. It is engraved on steel; and beautifully finished in a superb style of line and stipple;—mezzotinto being entirely rejected. It is forty inches by twenty-seven in size, and contains over sixty figures; comprising the members of the Council, and a number of the most distinguished characters of the day. Among the most conspicuous are Edmund Burke, Dr. Priestley, and Jeremy Bentham, and other personal friends of Franklin, who were at his side during the trying scene.

The portraits of the members of the Council, and the distinguished persons present are perfectly reliable. Many of them have never before been published; and were obtained especially for this work from drawings and paintings remaining in the possession of their families. Several years were devoted to procuring them, through the exertions of competent agents in London, and at an expense greater than is usually incurred for the *full completion* of meretricious engravings, which are frequently published in this country as works of art. The interior of the hall, with its furniture and decorations, is perfectly accurate in all its details.

The engraving is from a magnificent painting in oil, by C. Schuessele, of Philadelphia, seven feet by five in size, which, for masterly grouping, splendid arrangement of effect and color, and perfect accuracy of portraiture and costume, is universally conceded to be one of the finest national pictures in the country; and has excited the greatest attention wherever exhibited.

The entire work has been over eight years in preparation, and the best talent in the country employed in every department, that its intrinsic qualities as a work of art may be commensurate with its national and historical importance. It is confidently hoped that its publication will inaugurate an era in American art, when the efforts of our native artists will be produced in a style to meet the growing taste and refinement of the people, and vie with the best productions of the European masters.

The volume which accompanies the engraving is published exclusively for subscribers. It contains the splendid chapter from Bancroft's History of the United States descriptive of the event forming the subject of the picture; and the entire correspondence of Hutchinson and Oliver. The correspondence is from a volume which is now entirely out of print; and so extremely rare that it is difficult to find even in the largest and most complete libraries in the country. It is in itself an important historical work, and a valuable addition to the picture.

The Engraving and Book can only be obtained by subscription; and through the authorized agents of the publisher. In no event will it be on sale at the print or book stores.

CONTENTS.

	PAGE
THE KING IN COUNCIL INSULTS THE GREAT AMERICAN PLEBEIAN,	3
LETTERS OF HUTCHINSON AND OLIVER,	17
REMARKS IN DEFENCE OF THE FOREGOING LETTERS,	52
PROCEEDINGS ON THE ADDRESS OF THE ASSEMBLY OF MASSACHUSETTS BAY,	67
THE SPEECH OF THE RIGHT HONORABLE THE EARL OF CHATHAM, &c.,	122

THE KING IN COUNCIL INSULTS THE GREAT AMERICAN PLEBEIAN.

THE just man covered with the opprobrium of crime and meriting all the honors of virtue, is the sublimest spectacle that can appear on earth. Against Franklin were arrayed the Court, the Ministry, the Parliament, and an all-pervading social influence; but he only assumed a firmer demeanor and a loftier tone. On delivering to Lord Dartmouth the Address to the King for the removal of Hutchinson and Oliver, he gave assurances, that the people of Massachusetts aimed at no novelties; that, "having lately discovered the authors of their grievances to be some of their own people, their resentment against Britain was thence much abated." The Secretary promised at once to lay the Petition before the King, and expressed his "pleasure" at the communication, as well as his "earnest hope" for the restoration "of the most perfect tranquillity and happiness." It had been the unquestionable duty of the Agent of the Province to communicate proof that Hutchinson and Oliver were conspiring against its Constitution; to bring censure on the act, it was necessary to raise a belief that the evidence had been surreptitiously obtained. To that end Hutchinson was unwearied in his entreaties; but William Whately, the Banker, who was his brother's executor, was persuaded that the letters in question had never been in his hands, and refused to cast imputations on any one.

The newspaper Press was therefore employed to spread a rumor that they had been dishonestly obtained through John Temple. The anonymous calumny which was attributed to Bernard, Knox, and Mauduit, was denied by one calling himself "a Member of Parliament," who also truly affirmed, that the letters which were sent to Boston had never been in the executor's hands. Again the Press declared, what was also true, that Whately, the executor, had submitted files of his brother's letters to Temple's examination, who, it was insinuated, had seized the opportunity to purloin them. Temple repelled the charge instantly and successfully. Whately, the executor, never made a suggestion that the letters had been taken away by Temple, and always believed the contrary; but swayed not so much by the solicitations of Hutchinson and Mauduit, as by his sudden appointment as a banker to the Treasury, he published an evasive card, in which he did not relieve Temple from the implication.

A duel followed between Temple and Whately, without witnesses; then newspaper altercations on the incidents of the meeting; till another duel seemed likely to ensue. Cushing, the timid Speaker of the Massachusetts Assembly, to whom the letters had been officially transmitted, begged that he might not be known as having received them, lest it should be "a damage" to him; the Member of Parliament, who had had them in his possession, never permitted himself to be named; Temple, who risked offices producing a thousand pounds a year, publicly denied "any concern in procuring or transmitting them." To prevent bloodshed, Franklin assumed the undivided responsibility, from which every one else was disposed to shrink. " I," said he, " I alone am the person who obtained and transmitted to Boston the letters in question." His ingenuousness exposed him to " unmerited abuse" in every company and in every newspaper, and gave his enemies an opening to reject publicly the Petition; which otherwise would have been dismissed without parade.

On Tuesday the eleventh of January, Franklin for Massachusetts, and Mauduit, with Wedderburn, for Hutchinson and Oliver, appeared before the Privy Council. " I thought," said Franklin, " that this had been a matter of politics, and not of law, and have not brought any counsel." The hearing was, therefore, adjourned to Saturday the twenty-ninth. Meantime the Ministry and the courtiers expressed their rage against him; and talked of his dismissal from office, of his arrest, and imprisonment at Newgate; of a search among his papers for proofs of Treason; while Wedderburn openly professed the intention to inveigh personally against him. He was also harassed with a subpœna from the Chancellor, to attend his Court at the suit of William Whately, respecting the letters.

The public sentiment was, moreover, embittered by accounts that the Americans would not suffer the landing of the tea. The zeal of the Colonists was unabated. On New Year's eve, a half chest of tea, picked up in Roxbury, was burned on Boston Common; on the twentieth, three barrels of Bohea tea were burned in State Street. On the twenty-fifth, John Malcolm, a North Briton, who had been aid to Gov. Tryon in his war against the Regulators, and was now a preventive officer in the Customs, having indiscreetly provoked the populace, was seized, tarred and feathered, and paraded under the gallows.

The General Court also assembled, full of a determination to compel the Judges to refuse the salaries proffered by the King. Enough of the prevalence of this spirit was known in England, to raise a greater clamor against the Americans, than had ever before existed. Hypocrites, traitors, rebels, and villains, were the softest epithets applied to them; and some menaced war, and would have given full scope to sanguinary rancor. On the twenty-seventh, the Government received official information, that the people of Boston had thrown the tea overboard, and this event swelled the anger against the Americans.

In this state of public feeling, Franklin, on the twenty-ninth, assisted by Dunning and John Lee, came before the Privy Council, to advocate the removal of Hutchinson and Oliver, in whose behalf appeared Israel Mauduit, the old adviser of the Stamp Tax; and Wedderburn, the Solicitor General. It was a day of great expectation. Thirty-five Lords of the Council were present; a larger number than had ever attended a hearing; and the room was filled with a crowded audience, among whom were Priestley, Jeremy Bentham, and Edmund Burke.

The Petition and accompanying papers having been read, Dunning asked on the part of his clients the reason of his being ordered to attend. "No cause," said he, "is instituted; nor do we think advocates necessary; nor are they demanded on the part of the Colony. The Petition is not in the nature of accusation, but of advice and request. It is an Address to the King's wisdom, not an application for criminal justice; when referred to the Council, it is a matter for political prudence, not for judicial determination. The matter, therefore, rests wholly in your Lordship's opinion of the propriety or impropriety of continuing persons in authority, who are represented by legal bodies, competent to such representation, as having (whether on sufficient or insufficient grounds) entirely forfeited the confidence of the Assemblies whom they were to act with, and of the people whom they were to govern. The resolutions on which that representation is founded, lie before your Lordships, together with the letters from which they arose.

"If your Lordships should think that these actions, which appear to the Colony Representative to be faulty, ought in other places to appear meritorious, the Petition has not desired that the parties should be punished as criminals for these actions of supposed merit; nor even that they may not be rewarded. It only requests that these gentlemen may be removed to places where such merits are better understood, and such rewards may be more approved." He spoke well, and was seconded by Lee.

The question as presented by Dunning, was already decided in favor of the Petitioners; it was the universal opinion that Hutchinson ought to be superseded. Wedderburn changed the issue, as if Franklin were on trial; and in a speech which was a continued tissue of falsehood and ribaldry, turned his invective against the Petitioners and their Messenger. Of all men, Franklin was the most important in any attempt at conciliation. He was the Agent of the two great Colonies of Massachusetts and Pennsylvania, and also of New Jersey and Georgia; was the friend of Edmund Burke, who was agent for New York. All the troubles in British colonial policy had grown out of the neglect of his advice, and there was no one who could have mediated like him between the Metropolis and the Americans. He was now thrice venerable, from genius, fame in the world of science, and age, being already nearly threescore years and ten. This man Wedderburn, turning from the real question, employed all the cunning powers of distortion and misrepresentation to abuse. With an absurdity of application which the Lords of the Privy Council were too much prejudiced to observe, he drew a parallel between Boston and Capri, Hutchinson and Sejanus, the humble Petition of the Massachusetts Assembly, and a verbose and grand epistle of the Emperor Tiberius. Franklin, whose character was most benign, and who, from obvious motives of mercy, had assumed the sole responsibility of obtaining the letters, he described as a person of the most deliberate malevolence, realizing in life what poetic fiction only had penned for the breast of a bloody African. The speech of Hutchinson, challenging a discussion of the Supremacy of Parliament, had been not only condemned by public opinion in England, but disapproved by the Secretary of State; Wedderburn pronounced it "a masterly one," which had "stunned the faction." Franklin, for twenty years had exerted his wonderful powers as the great conciliator, had never once employed the American press to alarm the American people, but had sought to prevent the Parliamentary taxation of America, by private and successful remonstrance during the time of the Pelhams; by seasonable remonstrance with Grenville against the Stamp Act; by honest and true answers to the inquiries of the House of Commons; by the best of advice to Shelburne. When sycophants sought by flattery to mislead the Minister for America, he had given correct information and safe counsel to the Ministry of Grafton, and repeated it emphatically, and in writing, to the Ministry of North ; but Wedderburn stigmatized this wise and hearty lover of both countries as "a true incendiary." The letters which had been written by public men, in public offices, on public affairs, to one who formed an integral part of the body that had been declared to possess absolute power over America, and which had been written for the purpose of producing a tyrannical exercise of that absolute power, he called private. Hutchinson had solicited the place held by Franklin, from which Franklin was to be dismissed; this fact was suppressed, and the wanton falsehood substituted, that Franklin had desired the Governor's office, and had basely planned "his rival's overthrow." Franklin had inclosed the letters officially to the Speaker of the Massachusetts Assembly, without a single injunction of secrecy with regard to the sender; Wedderburn maintained that they were sent anonymously and secretly ; and by an argument founded on a mis-statement, but which he put forward as irrefragable, he pretended to convict Franklin of having obtained the letters by fraudulent and corrupt means, or of having stolen them from the person who stole them.

The Lords of Council as he spoke, cheered him on by their laughter ; and the cry of " Hear him, hear him," burst repeatedly from a body which professed to be sitting in judgment as the highest Court of Appeal for the Colonies, and yet encouraged the advocate of one of the parties to insult a public envoy, present only as the person delivering the Petition of a great and loyal Colony.

Meantime the gray-haired Franklin, whom Kant, the noblest philosopher of that age, had called the modern Prometheus, stood conspicuously erect, confronting his vilifier and the Privy Council, compelled to listen while calumny, in the service of lawless force, aimed a death-blow at his honor, and his virtues called on God and man to see how unjustly he suffered.

The reply of Dunning, who was very ill and was fatigued by standing so long, could scarcely be heard; and that of Lee produced no impression. There was but one place in England where fit reparation could be made; and there was but one man who had the eloquence and the courage and the weight of character to effect the atonement. For the present, Franklin must rely on the approval of the monitor within his own breast. "I have never been so sensible of the power of a good conscience," said he to Priestly; "for if I had not considered the thing for which I have been so much insulted, as one of the best actions of my life, and what I should certainly do again in the same circumstances, I could not have supported it." But it was not to him, it was to the people of Massachusetts, and to New England, and to all America, that the insult was offered through their Agent.

Franklin and Wedderburn parted; the one to spread the celestial fire of freedom among men; to make his name a cherished household word in every nation of Europe; and in the beautiful language of Washington, "to be venerated for benevolence, to be admired for talents, to be esteemed for patriotism, to be beloved for philanthropy;" the other childless, though twice wedded, unbeloved, wrangling with the patron who had impeached his veracity, busy only in " getting every thing he could" in the way of titles and riches, as the wages of corruption. Franklin, when he died, had nations for his mourners, and the great and the good throughout the world as his eulogists; when Wedderburn died, there was no man to mourn; no senate spoke his praise; no poet embalmed his memory; and his King, hearing that he was certainly dead, said only, " He has not left a greater knave behind him in my dominions." The report of the Lords, which had been prepared beforehand, was immediately signed; and " they went away, almost ready to throw up their hats for joy, as if by the vehement Philippic against the hoary-headed Franklin, they had obtained a triumph."

And who were the Lords of the Council, that thus thought to mark and brand the noblest representative of free labor who for many a year had earned his daily bread as apprentice, journeyman, or mechanic, and "knew the heart of the working man," and felt for the people, of whom he remained one ? If they who upon that occasion pretended to sit in judgment had never come into being, whom among them all would humanity have missed ? But how would it have suffered if Franklin had not lived !

The men in power who on that day sought to rob Franklin of his good name, wounded him on the next in his fortunes, by turning him out of his place in the British American Post Office. That institution had yielded no revenue till he organized it, and yielded none after his dismissal.

On Tuesday, the first of February, the Earl of Buckinghamshire, who had attended the Privy Council, went to the House of Lords, " to put the Ministry in mind that he was to be bought by private contract." Moving for the Boston Correspondence, he said, " The question is no longer about the liberty of North America, but whether we are to be free or slaves to our Colonies. Franklin is here, not as the Agent of a Province, but as an Ambassador from the States of America. His embassy to us is like nothing but that sent by Louis XIV. to the Republic of Genoa, commanding the doge to come and appease the Grand Monarch, by prostrating himself at Versailles." " Such language is wild," replied the Earl of Stair. " Humanity, commercial policy, and the public necessities dictate a very contrary one." " I would not throw cold water on the noble Lord's zeal," said the good Lord Dartmouth ; as he made the request that further despatches might be waited for.

Superior to injury, Franklin, or, as Rockingham called him, the " magnanimous " " old man," still sought for conciliation, and seizing the moment when he was sure of all sympathies, he wrote to his constituents to begin the work, by making compensation to the East India Company before any compulsive measures were thought of. But events were to proceed as they had been ordered. Various measures were talked of for altering the Constitution of the Government in Massachusetts, and for prosecuting individuals. The opinion in town was very general that America would submit ; that Government was taken by surprise when they repealed the Stamp Act, and that all might be recovered.

The King was obstinate, had no one near him to explain the true state of things in America, and admitted no misgivings except for not having sooner enforced the claims of authority. On the fourth day of February, he consulted the American Commander-in-Chief, who had recently returned from New York. "I am willing to go back at a day's notice," said Gage, "if coercive measures are adopted. They will be lions, while we are lambs; but if we take the resolute part, they will undoubtedly prove very meek. Four regiments sent to Boston will be sufficient to prevent any disturbance." The King received these opinions as certainly true; and wished their adoption. He would enforce the claim of authority at all hazards. "All men," said he, "now feel, that the fatal compliance in 1766 has increased the pretensions of the Americans to absolute independence." In the letters of Hutchinson, he saw nothing to which the least exception could be taken; and condemned the Address of Massachusetts, of which every word was true, as the production of " falsehood and malevolence."

Accordingly, on the seventh day of February, in the Court at St. James's, the report of the Privy Council was read, embodying the vile insinuations of Wedderburn; and the Petition which Franklin had presented, and which expressed the exact truth, was described as formed on false allegations, and was dismissed by the King as " groundless, vexatious, and scandalous."—*Bancroft's History of the United States.*

THE LETTERS OF

GOVERNOR HUTCHINSON AND LIEUTENANT GOVERNOR OLIVER,

WITH THE ASSEMBLY'S ADDRESS,

AND THE PROCEEDINGS OF THE LORDS' COMMITTEE OF COUNCIL;

WITH THE SPEECH OF MR. WEDDERBURN,

RELATING TO THOSE LETTERS;

AND THE REPORT OF THE LORDS' COMMITTEE

TO HIS MAJESTY IN COUNCIL;

AND THE SPEECH OF THE

EARL OF CHATHAM ON AMERICAN AFFAIRS

LONDON :
PRINTED FOR J. WILKIE,
AT 71 IN ST. PAUL'S CHURCH-YARD, 1774.

PHILADELPHIA :
RE-PRINTED BY JOHN M. BUTLER,
242 CHESTNUT STREET.
1860.

LETTERS, &C.

Boston, June 18, 1768.

Sir:—As you allow me the honor of your correspondence, I may not omit acquainting you with so remarkable an event as the withdraw of the Commissioners of the Customs, and most of the other officers under them, from the town on board the Romney, with an intent to remove from thence to the castle.

In the evening of the 10th, a sloop belonging to Mr. Hancock, a Representative for Boston, and a wealthy merchant of great influence over the populace, was seized by the Collector and Comptroller for a very notorious breach of the acts of trade, and, after seizure, taken into custody by the officer of the Romney man-of-war, and removed under command of her guns. It is pretended that the removal, and not the seizure, incensed the people. It seems not very material which it was. A mob was immediately raised, the officers insulted, bruised, and much hurt, and the windows of some of their houses broke; a boat belonging to the Collector burnt in triumph, and many threats uttered against the Commissioners and their officers: no notice being taken of their extravagance in the time of it, nor any endeavors by any authority, except the Governor, the next day, to discover and punish the offenders; and there being a rumor of a higher mob intended Monday (the 13th) in the evening, the Commissioners, four of them, thought themselves altogether unsafe, being destitute of protection, and removed with their families to the Romney, and there remain and hold their board, and next week intend to do the same, and also open the custom house at the castle. The Governor pressed the council to assist him with their advice, but they declined and evaded, calling it a brush, or small disturbance by boys and negroes, not considering how much it must be resented in England that the officers of the crown should think themselves obliged to quit the place of their residence, and go on board a King's ship for safety, and all the internal authority of the province take no notice of it. The town of Boston have had repeated meetings, and by their votes declared the Commissioners and their officers a great grievance, and yesterday instructed their Representatives to endeavor, that enquiry should be made by the Assembly whether any person by writing or in any other way, had encouraged the sending troops here, there being some alarming reports that troops are expected, but have not taken any measures to discountenance the promoters of the late proceedings; but, on the contrary, appointed one or more of the actors or abettors on a committee appointed to wait on the Governor, and to desire him to order the man-of-war out of the harbor.

Ignorant as they be, yet the heads of a Boston town-meeting influence all public measures.

It is not possible this anarchy should last always. Mr. Hallowell, who will be the bearer of this, tells me he has the honor of being personally known to you. I beg leave to refer you to him for a more full account.

I am, with great esteem, Sir,
Your most humble and obedient servant,
Tho. Hutchinson.

Boston, August, 1768.

Sir :—It is very necessary other information should be had in England of the present state of the commissioners of the customs than what common fame will bring to you, or what you will receive from most of the letters which go from hence, people in general being prejudiced by many false reports and misrepresentations concerning them. Seven-eighths of the people of the country suppose the board itself to be unconstitutional, and cannot be undeceived and brought to believe that a board has existed in England all this century, and that the board established here has no new powers given to it. Our incendiaries know it, but they industriously and very wickedly publish the contrary. As much pains have been taken to prejudice the country against the persons of the Commissioners, and their characters have been misrepresented and cruelly treated, especially since their confinement at the castle, where they are not so likely to hear what is said of them, and are not so able to confute it.

It is now pretended they need not to have withdrawn, that Mr. Williams had stood his ground without any injury. although the mob beset his house, &c. There never was that spirit raised against the under officers as against the Commissioners, I mean four of them. They had a public affront offered them by the town of Boston, who refused to give the use of their hall for a public dinner, unless it was stipulated that the Commissioners should not be invited. An affront of the same nature at the motion of Mr. Hancock was offered by a company of cadets. Soon after a vessel of Mr. Hancock's being seized, the officers were mobbed, and the Commissioners were informed they were threatened. I own I was in pain for them. I do not believe if the mob had seized them, there was any authority able and willing to have rescued them. After they had withdrawn, the town signified to the Governor by a message that it was expected or desired they should not return. It was then the general voice that it would not be safe for them to return. After all this, the sons of liberty say they deserted or abdicated.

The other officers of the customs in general either did not leave the town, or soon returned to it. Some of them seem to be discontented with the Commissioners. Great pains have been taken to increase the discontent. Their office by these means is rendered extremely burdensome. Every thing they do is found fault with, and yet no particular illegality or even irregularity mentioned. There is too much hauteur, some of their officers say, in the treatment they receive. They say, they treat their officers as the Commissioners treat their officers in England, and require no greater deference. After all, it is not the persons, but the office of the Commissioners which has raised this spirit, and the distinction made between the Commissioners, is because it has been given out that four of them were in favor of the new establishment, and the fifth was not. If Mr. Hallowell arrived safe, he can inform you many circumstances relative to this distinction, which I very willingly excuse myself from mentioning.

I know of no burden brought upon the fair trader by the new establishment. The illicit trader finds the risk greater than it used to be, especially in the port where the board is constantly held. Another circumstance which increases the prejudice is this; the new duties happened to take place just about the time the Commissioners arrived. People have absurdly connected the duties and Board of Commissioners, and suppose we should have had no additional duties, if there had been no Board to have the charge of collecting them. With all the aid you can give to the officers of the crown, they will have enough to do to maintain the authority of government, and to carry the laws into execution. If they are discountenanced, neglected, or fail of support from you, they must submit to every thing the present opposers of government think fit to require of them.

There is no office under greater discouragements than that of the Commissioners. Some of my friends recommended me to the ministry. I think myself very happy that I am not one. Indeed it would have been incompatible with my post as chief justice, and I must have declined it, and I should do it, although no greater salary had been affixed to the chief justice's place, than the small pittance allowed by the province.

From my acquaintance with the Commissioners I have conceived a personal esteem for them, but my chief inducement to make this representation to you, is a regard to the public interest, which I am sure will suffer if the opposition carry their point against them.

I am, with very great esteem, Sir,
Your most obedient humble servant,
Tho. Hutchinson.

August 10. Yesterday at a meeting of the merchants, it was agreed by all present to give no more orders for goods from England, nor receive any on commission until the late acts are repealed. And it is said all except sixteen in the town have subscribed an engagement to that tenor. I hope the subscription will be printed, that I may transmit it to you.

Boston, October 4, 1768.

Dear Sir :—I was absent upon one of our circuits when Mr. Byles arrived. Since my return, I have received from him your obliging letter of 31st July. I never dared to think what the resentment of the nation would be upon Hallowell's arrival. It is not strange that measures should be immediately taken to reduce the colonies to their former state of government and order, but that the national funds should be affected by it, is to me a little mysterious and surprising. Principles of government absurd enough spread through all the colonies; but I cannot think that in any colony, people of any consideration have ever been so mad as to think of a revolt. Many of the common people have been in a frenzy, and talked of dying in defence of their liberties, and have spoke and printed what is highly criminal, and too many of rank above the vulgar, and some in public posts have countenanced and encouraged them, until they increased so much in their numbers, and in their opinion of their importance, as to submit to government no further than they thought proper. The legislative powers have been influenced by them, and the executive powers entirely lost their force. There has been continual danger of mobs and insurrections, but they would have spent all their force within ourselves, the officers of the crown, and some of the few friends who dared to stand by them, possibly might have been knocked on the head, and some such fatal event would probably have brought the people to their senses. For four or five weeks past the distemper has been growing, and I confess I have not been without some apprehensions for myself, but my friends have had more for me; and I have heard repeated and frequent notices from them from different quarters, one of the last I will inclose to you.* In this state of things, there was no security, but quitting my posts, which nothing but the last extremity would justify. As Chief Justice, for two years after our first disorders, I kept the grand juries tolerably well to their duty. The last spring, there had been several riots, and a most infamous libel had been published in one of the papers, which I enlarged upon, and the grand jury had determined to make presentments, but the Attorney-General not attending them the first day, Otis and his creatures, who were alarmed and frightened, exerted themselves the next day, and prevailed upon so many of the jury to change their voices, that there was not a sufficient number left to find a bill. They have been ever since more enraged against me than ever. At the desire of the Governor I committed to wri-

* See the following Letter.

ting the charge while it lay in my memory, and as I have no further use for it, I will inclose it, as it may give you some idea of our judicatories.

Whilst we were in this state, news came of two regiments being ordered from Halifax, and soon after two more from Ireland. The minds of people were more and more agitated, broad hints were given that the troops should never land, a barrel of tar was placed upon the beacon, in the night to be fired, to bring in the country, when the troops appeared, and all the authority of the government was not strong enough to remove it. The town of Boston met and passed a number of weak, but very criminal votes; and as the Governor declined calling an Assembly, they sent circular letters to all the towns and districts to send a person each that there might be a general consultation at so extraordinary a crisis. They met and spent a week, made themselves ridiculous, and then dissolved themselves, after a message or two to the Governor, which he refused to receive; a petition to the King, which I dare say their agent will never be allowed to present, and a result which they published ill-natured and impotent.

In this confusion the troops from Halifax arrived. I never was much afraid of the people's taking arms, but I was apprehensive of violence from the mob, it being their last chance before the troops could land. As the prospect of revenge became more certain, their courage abated in proportion. Two regiments are landed, but a new grievance is now raised. The troops are by act of parliament to be quartered no where else but in the barracks, until they are full. There are barracks enough at the castle to hold both regiments. It is therefore against the

Act to bring any of them into the town. This was started by the Council in their answer to the Governor, which, to make themselves popular, they in an unprecedented way published and have alarmed all the province; for although none but the most contracted minds could put such a construction upon the act, yet after this declaration of the Council, nine-tenths of the people suppose it just. I wish the act had been better expressed, but it is absurd to suppose the parliament intended to take from the King the direction of his forces, by confining them to a place where any of the colonies might think fit to build barracks. It is besides ungrateful, for it is known to many that this provision was brought into the bill after it had been framed without it, from mere favor to the colonies. I hear the Commander-in-Chief has provided barracks or quarters, but a doubt still remains with some of the Council, whether they are to furnish the articles required, unless the men are in the province barracks, and they are to determine upon it to-day.

The government has been so long in the hands of the populace, that it must come out of them by degrees, at least it will be a work of time to bring the people back to just notions of the nature of government.

Mr. Pepperrell, a young gentleman of good character, and grandson and principal heir to the late Sir William Pepperrell, being bound to London, I shall deliver this letter to him, as it will be too bulky for postage, and desire him to wait upon you with it.

I am, with very great esteem, Sir,
    Your most humble and most obedient servant,
                          Tho. Hutchinson.

Sir:—The great esteem I have for you in every point of light, perhaps renders my fears and doubts for the safety of your person greater than they ought to be; however if that is an error, it certainly results from true friendship, naturally jealous. Last night, I was informed by a gentleman of my acquaintance, who had his information from one intimate with and knowing to the infernal purposes of the sons of liberty, as they falsely style themselves, that he verily believed, from the terrible threats and menaces by those Catilines against you, that your life is greatly in danger. This informant, I know, is under obligations to you, and is a man of veracity. He expressed himself with concern for you, and the gentleman acquainting me with this horrid circumstance, assured me he was very uneasy till you had notice. I should have done myself the honor of waiting on you, but am necessarily prevented. The duty I owed to you as a friend, and to the public as a member of society, would not suffer me to rest till I had put your honor upon your guard; for though this may be a false alarm, nothing would have given me greater pain, if any accident had happened, and I had been silent. If possible, I will see you to-morrow, and let you know further into this black affair. And am, with the sincerest friendship and respect, your Honor's

Most obedient, and most humble servant,

Rob. Auchmuty.

To the hon'ble Thomas Hutchinson, Sept. 14, 1768.

Boston, Dec. 10, 1768.

Dear Sir:—I am just now informed that a number of

the Council, perhaps eight or ten, who live in and near this town, have met together and agreed upon a long address or petition to Parliament, and that it will be sent by this ship to Mr. Bollan to be presented. Mr. Danforth, who is President of the Council, told the Governor, upon enquiry, that it was sent to him to sign, and he supposed the rest of the Council who had met together, would sign after him in order; but he had since found that they had wrote over his name, by order of Council, which makes it appear to be an act of Council. This may be a low piece of cunning in him, but be it as it may, it is proper it should be known, that the whole is no more than the doings of a part of the Council only; although even that is not very material, since, if they had all been present, without the Governor's summons, the meeting would have been irregular and unconstitutional, and ought to be discountenanced and censured. I suppose there is no instance of the Privy Council's meeting and doing business without the King's presence or special direction, except in committees upon such business as by his Majesty's order has been referred to them by an act of Council; and I have no instance here without the Governor, until within three or four months past.

I thought it very necessary the circumstances of this proceeding should be known, though if there be no necessity for it, I think it would be best it should not be known that the intelligence comes from me.

I am, with very great regard, Sir,
Your most humble and most obedient servant,
THO. HUTCHINSON.

Boston, Jan. 20, 1769.

DEAR SIR :—You have laid me under very great obligations by the very clear and full account of proceedings in Parliament, which I received from you by Capt. Scott. You have also done much service to the people of the province. For a day or two after the ship arrived, the enemies of government gave out that their friends in Parliament were increasing, and all things would be soon on the old footing ; in other words, that all acts imposing duties would be repealed, the Commissioners' board dissolved, the customs put on the old footing, and *illicit* trade be carried on with little or no hazard. It was very fortunate that I had it in my power to prevent such a false representation from spreading through the province. I have been very cautious of using your name, but I have been very free in publishing abroad the substance of your letter, and declaring that I had my intelligence from the best authority, and have in a great measure defeated the ill design in raising and attempting to spread so groundless a report. What marks of resentment the Parliament will show, whether they will be upon the province in general, or particular persons, is extremely uncertain, but that they will be placed somewhere is most certain ; and I add, because I think it ought to be so, that those who have been most steady in preserving the constitution and opposing the licentiousness of such as call themselves Sons of Liberty, will certainly meet with favor and encouragement.

This is most certainly a crisis. I really wish that there may not have been the least degree of severity beyond what is absolutely necessary to maintain, I think I may say to you, the dependance which a colony ought to have upon the present state; but if no measures shall have been taken to secure this dependance, or nothing more than some declaratory acts or resolves, it is all over with us. The friends of government will be utterly disheartened, and the friends of anarchy will be afraid of nothing, be it ever so extravagant.

The last vessel from London had a quick passage. We expect to be in suspense for the three or four next weeks, and then to hear our fate. I never think of the measures necessary for the peace and good order of the colonies without pain. There must be an abridgment of what are called English liberties. I relieve myself by considering that in a remove from the state of nature to the most perfect state of government, there must be a great restraint of natural liberty. I doubt whether it is possible to project a system of government in which a colony 3000 miles distant from the parent state shall enjoy all the liberty of the parent state. I am certain I have never yet seen the projection. I wish the good of the colony when I wish to see some further restraint of liberty, rather than the connection with the parent state should be broken; for I am sure such a breach must prove the ruin of the colony. Pardon me this excursion, it really proceeds from the state of mind into which our perplexed affairs often throws me.

I have the honor to be, with very great esteem, Sir, your most humble and most obedient servant,

THO. HUTCHINSON.

Boston, October 26, 1769.

DEAR SIR :—I thank you for your last favor of July

18th. I fancy in my last to you, about two months ago, I have answered the greatest part of it.

My opinion upon the combination of the merchants, I gave you very fully. How long they will be able to continue them if Parliament should not interpose, is uncertain. In most articles they may another year, and you run the risk of their substituting, when they are put to their shifts, something of their own in the place of what they used to have from you, and which they will never return to you for. But it is not possible that provision for dissolving these combinations, and subjecting all who do not renounce them to penalties adequate to the offence, should not be made the first week the parliament meets. Certainly all parties will unite in so extraordinary a case, if they never do in any other. So much has been said upon the repeal of the duties laid by the last act, that it will render it very difficult to keep people's minds quiet, if that should be refused them. They deserve punishment, you will say; but laying or continuing taxes upon all cannot be thought equal, seeing many will be punished who are not offenders. Penalties of another kind seem better adapted.

I have been tolerably treated since the Governor's departure, no other charge being made against me in our scandalous newspapers, except my bad principles in matters of government; and this charge has had little effect, and a great many friends promise me support.

I must beg the favor of you to keep secret every thing I write, until we are in a more settled state, for the party here, either by their agent, or by some of their emissaries in London, have sent them every report or rumor of the contents of letters wrote from hence. I hope we shall see better times both here and in England.

I am, with great esteem, Sir,
Your most obedient servant,
THO. HUTCHINSON.

Boston, May 7, 1767.

SIR:—I am indebted to you for the obliging manner in which you received my recommendation of my good friend Mr. Paxton, as well as for the account you are pleased to send me of the situation of affairs in the mother country.

I am very sorry that the colonies give you so much employment, and it is impossible to say how long it will be before things settle into quiet among us. We have some here who have been so busy in fomenting the late disturbances, that they may now think it needful for their own security to keep up the spirit. They have plumed themselves much upon the victory they have gained, and the support they have since met with; nor could any thing better show what they would still be at, than the manner in which, by their own account published in the newspapers last August, they celebrated the 14th of that month, as the first anniversary commemoration of what they had done at the tree of Liberty on that day the year before. Here a number of respectable gentlemen, as they inform us, now met, and among other toasts drank General Paoli, and the spark of liberty kindled in Spain. I am now speaking of a few individuals only, the body of the people are well disposed; yet when you come to see the journal of the House of Representatives the last session, I fear you will think that the same spirit has seized our public counsels. I can, however, fairly say thus much in behalf of the government, that the last house was packed by means of a public proscription just before the election, of the greatest part of those who had appeared in the preceding session in the support of government: their names were published in an inflammatory newspaper, and their constituents made to believe they were about to sell them for slaves. Writs are now out for a new Assembly, but I cannot answer for the choice: I hope, however, that the people in general are in a better temper; yet the moderate men have been so brow-beaten in the House, and found themselves so insignificant there the last year, that some of them will voluntarily decline coming again. I think this looks too much like a despair of the commonwealth, and cannot be justified on patriotic principles.

The election of Counsellors was carried the last year as might have been expected from such an house. The officers of the crown, and the judges of the superior court were excluded. And I hear that it is the design of some, who expect to be returned members of the house this year, to make sure work at the ensuing election of Counsellors, by excluding, if they can, the gentlemen of the Council (who by charter remain such till others are chosen in their room) from any share in the choice, though they have always had their voice in it hitherto from the first arrival of the charter. If the house do this, they will have it in their power to model the Council as they please, and throw all the powers of government into the hands of the people, unless the Governor should again exert his negative as he did the last year.

You have doubtless seen some of the curious messages from the late house to the Governor, and can't but have observed with how little decency they have attacked both the Governor and the Lieutenant Governor. They have also in effect forced the Council to declare themselves parties in the quarrel they had against the latter in a matter of mere indifference. In their message to the Governor of the 21st of January, they have explicitly charged the Lieutenant Governor (a gentleman to whom they are more indebted than to any one man in the government) with "ambition and lust of power," merely for paying a compliment to the Governor agreeable to ancient usage, by attending him to court, and being present in the council-chamber when he made his speech at the opening of the session; at which time they go on to say, "none but the general court and their servants are intended to be present," still holding out to the people the servants of the crown as objects of insignificance, ranking the Secretary with their door-keeper, as servants of the Assembly; for the Secretary with his clerks and the door-keeper, are the only persons present with the Assembly on these occasions.

The officers of the crown being thus lessened in the eyes of the people, takes off their weight and influence, and the balance will of course turn in favor of the people, and what makes them still more insignificant is their dependance on the people for a necessary support: If something were left to the good-will of the people, yet nature should be sure of a support. The Governor's salary has for about thirty-five years past been pretty well understood to be £1000 a year sterling. When this sum was first agreed to, it was very well; but an increase of wealth since has brought along with it an increase of luxury, so that what was sufficient to keep up a proper distinction and support the dignity of a Governor then, may well be supposed to be insufficient for the purpose now. The Lieutenant Governor has no appointments as such: the Captaincy of Castle-William, which may be worth £120 sterling a year, is looked upon indeed as an appendage to his commission, and the late Lieutenant Governor enjoyed no other appointment: he lived a retired life upon his own estate in the country, and was easy. The present Lieutenant Governor indeed has other appointments, but the people are quarreling with him for it, and will not suffer him to be easy unless he will retire also.

The Secretary may have something more than £200 a year sterling, but has for the two last years been allowed £60 lawful money a year less than had been usual for divers years preceding, though he had convinced the house by their Committee, that without this deduction he would have had no more than £250 sterling per annum in fees, perquisites, and salary altogether, which is not the one half of his annual expense.

The crown did by charter reserve to itself the appointment of a Governor, Lieutenant Governor, and Secretary; the design of this was without doubt to maintain some kind of balance between the powers of the crown and of the people; but, if officers are not in some measure independent of the people (for it is difficult to serve two masters), they will sometimes have a hard struggle between duty to the crown and a regard to self, which must be a very disagreeable situation to them, as well as a weakening to the authority of government. The officers of the crown are very few, and are therefore the more easily provided for without burdening the people : and such provision I look upon as necessary to the restoration and support of the King's authority.

But it may be said, How can any new measures be taken without raising new disturbances ? The manufacturers in England, will rise again and defeat the measures of government. This game, 'tis true, has been played once and succeeded, and it has been asserted here, that it is in the power of the colonies at any time to raise a rebellion in England, by refusing to send for their manufactures.

For my own part, I do not believe this. The merchants in England, and I don't know but those in London and Bristol only, might always govern in this matter and quiet the manufacturer. The merchant's view is always to his own interest. As the trade is now managed, the dealer here sends to the merchant in England for his goods, upon these goods the English merchant puts a profit of 10 or more, probably 15 per cent. when he sends them to his employer in America. The merchant is so jealous of foregoing this profit, that an American trader cannot well purchase the goods he wants of the manufacturer ; for should the merchant know that the manufacturer had supplied an American, he would take off no more of his wares. The merchants therefore having this profit in view, will by one means or other secure it. They know the goods which the American market demands, and may therefore safely take them off from the manufacturer, though they should have no orders for shipping them this year or perhaps the next; and I dare say, it would not be longer before the Americans would clamor for a supply of goods from England, for it is vain to think they can supply themselves. The merchant might then put an advanced price upon his goods, and possibly be able to make his own terms; or if it should be thought the goods would not bear an advanced price to indemnify him, it might be worth while for the government to agree with the merchants beforehand to allow them a premium equivalent to the advance of their stock, and then the game would be over.

I have wrote with freedom, in confidence of my name's not being used on the occasion. For though I have wrote nothing but what in my conscience I think an American may upon just principles advance, and what a servant of the Crown ought upon all proper occasions to suggest, yet the many prejudices I have to combat with, may render it unfit it should be made public.

I communicated to Governor Bernard what you mentioned concerning him, who desires me to present you his compliments, and let you know that he is obliged to you for the expressions of your regard for his injured character.

I am, with great respect, Sir,
    Your most obedient and most humble servant,
        ANDREW OLIVER.

I ask your acceptance of a journal of the last session, which is put up in a box directed to the Secretary of the Board of trade.

Boston, May 11, 1768.

SIR:—I am at this moment favored with your very obliging letter by Capt. Jarvis, of the 2d March, which I have but just time to acknowledge, as this is the day given out for the ship to sail. I wrote you the 23d of February in reply to your letter of the 28th December; that of the 12th February which you refer to in this of the 2d of March is not yet come to hand. You lay me, Sir, under the greatest obligations, as well for the interesting account of public affairs, which you are from time to time pleased to transmit me, as for your steady attention to my private concerns. I shall always have the most grateful sense of Mr. Grenville's intentions of favor also, whether I ever reap any benefit from them or not. Without a proper support afforded to the King's officers, the respect due to government will of course fail; yet I cannot say whether, under the present circumstances, and considering the temper the people are now in, an additional provision for me would be of real benefit to me personally or not. It has been given out, that no person who receives a stipend from the government at home, shall live in the country. Government here wants some effectual support. No sooner was it known that the Lieutenant Governor had a provision of £200 a year made for him out of the revenue, than he was advised in the Boston Gazette to resign all pretensions to a seat in council, either with or without a voice. The temper of the people will be surely learnt from that infamous paper; it is the very thing that forms their temper; for if they are not in the temper of the writer at the time of the publication, yet it is looked upon as the ORACLE, and they soon bring their temper to it. Some of the latest of them are very expressive; I will not trouble you with sending them, as I imagine they some how or other find their way to you. But I cannot but apprehend from these papers, and from hints that are thrown out, that if the petition of the House to his Majesty, and their letters to divers noble Lords should fail of success, some people will be mad enough to go to extremities. The Commissioners of the Customs have already been openly affronted, the Governor's company of Cadets have come to a resolution not to wait on him (as usual) on the day of General Election, the 25th instant, if those gentlemen are of the company. And the Town of Boston have passed a Vote that Faneuil Hall (in which the Governor and his company usually dine on that day) shall not be opened to him, if the Commissioners are invited to dine with him. A list of Counsellors has within a few days past been printed and dispersed by way of sneer on Lord Shelburne's letter, made up of King's officers; which list, the writer says, if adopted at the next general election, may take away all grounds of complaint, and may possibly prove a healing and a very salutary measure. The Lieutenant Governor is at the head of this list, they have done me the honor to put me next; the Commissioners of the Customs are all in the list except Mr. Temple, and to complete the list, they have added some of the waiters. I never thought till very lately that they acted upon any settled plan, nor do I now think they have till of late; a few, a very few among us, have planned the present measures, and the government has been too weak to subdue their turbulent spirits. Our situation is not rightly known : but it is a matter worthy of the most serious attention.

I am, with the greatest respect, Sir,
    Your most obedient and most humble servant,
        ANDREW OLIVER.

I shall take proper care to forward your letter to Mr. Ingersol. He had received your last.

Boston, February 13, 1769.

SIR :—I have your very obliging favor of the 4th of October. I find myself constrained, as well by this letter as by my son and daughter Spooner's letters since, to render you my most sincere thanks for the very polite notice you have taken of them ; and I pray my most respectful compliments to the good lady, your mother, whose friendly reception of them at Nonsuch has, I find, engaged their warmest esteem and respect—He hath wrote us that he had a prospect of succeeding in the business he went upon ; but the last letter we had was from her of the 23d of November, acquainting us that he had been very ill, but was getting better. She writes as a person overcome with a sense of the kindness they had met with, in a place where they were strangers, on this trying occasion.

You have heard of the arrival of the King's troops; the quiet reception they met with among us was not at all surprising to me. I am sorry there was any occasion for sending them. From the address of the Gentlemen of the Council to General Gage, it might be supposed there was none. I have seen a letter from our friend Ingersoll with this paraphrase upon it—"We hope that your Excellency observing with your own eyes, now the troops are among us, our peaceable and quiet behavior, will be convinced that that wicked G———r B———d told a fib in saying, We were not so before they came."

I have given you the sense of a stranger on a single paragraph of this address, because I suspected my own opinion of it, till I found it thus confirmed. If you have the newspapers containing the address, your own good sense will lead you to make some other remarks upon it, as well as to trace the influence under which it seems to have been penned. The disturbers of our peace take great advantage of such aids, from people in office and power. The Lieutenant Governor has communicated to me your letter, containing an account of the debates in parliament, on the first day of the session. We soon expect their decision on American affairs, some I doubt not with fear and trembling. Yet I have very lately had occasion to know, that be the determination of parliament what it will, it is the determination of some to agree to no terms that shall remove us from our old foundation. This confirms me in an opinion, that I have taken up a long time since, that if there be no way to take off the original incendiaries, they will continue to instill their poison into the minds of the people, through the vehicle of the BOSTON GAZETTE.

In your letter to the Lieutenant Governor, you observe upon two defects in our constitution, the popular election of the Council, and the return of Juries by the Towns. The first of these arises from the Charter itself; the latter from our provincial Laws. The method of appointing our Grand Juries lies open to management.

Whoever pleases, nominates them at our town-meetings; by this means one who was supposed to be a principal in the Riots of the 10th of June last, was upon that Jury, whose business it was to inquire into them. But the provincial legislature hath made sufficient provision for the return of Petit Juries by their act of 23d Geo. 2d, which requires the several towns to take lists of all persons liable by law to serve, and forming them into two classes, put their names written on separate papers into two different boxes, one for the superior court, and the other for the inferior. And when venires are issued, the number therein required are to be drawn out in open town-meeting, no person to serve oftener than once in three years. The method of appointing Grand Juries appears indeed defective; but if the other is not, it may be imputed to the times rather than to the defect of the laws, that neither the Grand Juries nor the Petit Juries have of late answered the expectations of government.

As to the appointment of the Council, I am of opinion that neither the popular elections in this province, nor their appointment in what are called the royal governments by the King's mandamus, are free from exceptions, especially if the Council as a legislative body is intended to answer the idea of the House of Lords in the British legislature. There they are supposed to be a free and independent body, and on their being such, the strength and firmness of the constitution does very much depend: whereas the election or appointment of the Councils in the manner before-mentioned, renders them altogether dependent on their constituents. The King is the fountain of honor, and as such the peers of the realm derive their honors from him; but then they hold them by a surer tenure than the provincial Counsellors, who are appointed by mandamus. On the other hand, our popular elections very often expose them to contempt; for nothing is more common, than for the representatives, when they find the Council a little untractable at the close of the year, to remind them that May is at hand.

It may be accounted by the colonies as dangerous to admit of any alterations in their charters, as it is by the Governors in the church to make any in the establishment; yet to make the resemblance as near as may be to the British Parliament, some alteration is necessary.

It is not requisite, that I know of, that a Counsellor should be a Freeholder; his residence according to the charter, is a sufficient qualification; for that provides only, that he be an inhabitant of or proprietor of lands within the district for which he is chosen: whereas the Peers of the realm sit in the House of Lords, as I take it, in virtue of their baronies. If there should be a reform of any of the colony charters, with a view to keep up the resemblance of the three estates in England, the legislative Council should consist of men of landed estates: but as our landed estates here are small at present, the yearly value of £100 sterling per annum, might in some of them at least be a sufficient qualification. As our estates are partable after the decease of the proprietor, the honor could not be continued in families as in England. It might however be continued in the appointee *quam diu bene se gesserit*, and proof be required of some malpractice before a suspension or removal. Bankruptcy also might be another ground for removal. A small legislative Council might answer the purposes of government; but it might tend to weaken that leveling principle, which is cherished by the present popular constitution, to have an honorary order established, out of which the Council should be appointed. There is no way now to put a man of fortune above the common level, and exempt him from being chosen by the people into the lower offices, but his being appointed a Justice of the Peace; this is frequently done, when there is no kind of expectation of his undertaking the trust, and has its inconveniences. For remedy hereof it might be expedient to have an order of Patricians or Esquires instituted, to be all men of fortune or good landed estates, and appointed by the Governor with the advice of Council, and enrolled in the Secretary's office, who should be exempted from the lower offices in government, as the justices now are; and to have the legislative Council (which in the first instance might be nominated by the Crown) from time to time filled up, as vacancies happen, out of this order of men, who, if the order consisted only of men of landed estates, might elect, as the Scottish Peers do, only reserving to the King's Governor, a negative on such choice. The King in this case would be still acknowledged as the fountain of honor, as having, in the first instance, the appointment of the persons enrolled, out of whom the Council are to be chosen, and finally having a negative on the choice. Or, the King might have the immediate appointment by mandamus, as at present in the royal governments. As the gentlemen of the Council would rank above the body from which they are taken, they might bear a title one degree above that of Esquire. Besides this legislative Council, a privy Council might be established, to consist of some or all of those persons who constitute the legislative Council, and of other persons members of the

House of Representatives, or otherwise of note or distinction ; which would extend the honors of government, and afford opportunity of distinguishing men of character and reputation, the expectation of which would make government more respectable.

I would not trouble you with these reveries of mine, were I not assured of your readiness to forgive the communication, although you could apply it to no good purpose.

Mr. Spooner sent me a pamphlet under a blank cover, entitled, "*the state of the nation.*" I run over it by myself before I had heard any one mention it, and thought I could evidently mark the sentiments of some of my friends. By what I have since heard and seen, it looks as if I was not mistaken. Your right honorable friend I trust will not be offended if I call him mine—I am sure you will not when I term you such. I have settled it for a long time in my own mind, that without a representation in the supreme legislature, there cannot be that union between the head and the members as to produce a healthful constitution of the whole body. I have doubted whether this union could be perfected by the first experiment. The plan here exhibited seems to be formed in generous and moderate principles, and bids the fairest of any I have yet seen to be adopted. Such a great design may, as in painting, require frequent touching before it becomes a piece highly finished ; and after all, may require the meliorating hand of time to make it please universally. Thus the British constitution, considered as without the colonies, attained its glory. The book I had sent me is in such request, that I have not been able to keep it long enough by me, to consider it in all its parts.

I wish to hear how it is received in the House of Commons. I find by the publications, both of Governor Pownall and Mr. Bollan, that they each of them adopt the idea of an union and representation, and I think it must more and more prevail. The argument against it from local inconveniency, must, as it appears to me, be more than balanced by greater inconveniences on the other side the question : the great difficulty will be in the terms of union. I add no more, as I fear I have already trespassed much on your time and patience, but that I am, Sir,

Your obliged and most obedient humble servant,
ANDREW OLIVER.

New York, August 12, 1769.

SIR:—I have been in this city for some time past executing (with others) his Majesty's commission for settling the boundary between this province and that of New Jersey. I left Boston the 11th July, since which, my advices from London have come to me very imperfect ; but as my friend Mr. Thompson writes me, that he had drawn up my case, and with your approbation laid it before the D. of Grafton, I think it needful once more to mention this business to you.

There was a time when I thought the authority of government might have been easily restored ; but while its friends and the officers of the crown are left to an abject dependence on those very people who are undermining its authority ; and while these are suffered not only to go unpunished, but on the contrary, meet with all kind of support and encouragement, it cannot be expected that you will ever again recover that respect, which the colonies had been wont to pay to the parent state. Government at home will deceive itself, if it imagines that the taking off the duty on glass, paper, and painters' colors, will work a reconciliation, and nothing more than this, as I can learn, is proposed in Ld. H.'s late circular letter. It is the principle that is now disputed; the combination against importation extends to tea, although it comes cheaper than ever, as well to the other forementioned articles. In Virginia it is extended lately to wines: and I have heard one of the first leaders in these measures in Boston say, that we should never be upon a proper footing till all the revenue acts from the 15th Charles II. were repealed. Our Assembly in the Massachusetts may have been more illiberal than others in their public messages and resolves; yet we have some people among us still who dare to speak in favor of government. But here I do not find so much as one, unless it be some of the King's servants; and yet my business here leads me to associate with the best. They universally approve of the combination against importing of goods from Great Britain, unless the revenue acts are repealed, which appears to me little less than assuming a negative on all acts of parliament which they do not like! They say expressly, we are bound by none made since our emigration, but such as for our own convenience we choose to submit to; such, for instance, as that for establishing a post-office. The Bill of Rights and the Habeas Corpus Acts, they say, are only declaratory of common law, which we brought with us.

Under such circumstances as these, why should I wish to expose myself to popular resentment? Were I to receive any thing out of the revenue, I must expect to be abused for it. Nor do I find that our Chief Justice has received the £200 granted him for that service; and yet the Assembly have this year withheld his usual grant, most probably because he has such a warrant from the crown.

With regard to my negotiations with Mr. Rogers, I did in conformity to your opinion make an apology to Mr. Secretary Pownall for mentioning it, and there submitted it. I hear it has been since talked of; but unless I could be assured in one shape or other of £300 per annum, with the other office, I would not choose to quit what I have. I have no ambition to be distinguished, if I am only to be held up as a mark of popular envy or resentment. I was in hopes before now, through the intervention of your good offices, to have received some mark of favor from your good friend; but the time is not yet come to expect it through that channel! I will however rely on your friendship, whenever you can with propriety appear in forwarding my interest, or preventing any thing that may prove injurious to it.

If Mr. R. has interest enough to obtain the Secretary's place, I shall upon receiving proper security think myself in honor bound to second his views, though I have none at present from him but a conditional note he formerly wrote me. If he is not like to succeed, and my son Daniel could have my place, I would be content, unless affairs take a different turn, to resign in his favor, whether administration should think proper to make any further provision for me or not. And yet I never thought of withdrawing myself from the service, while there appeared to me any prospect of my being able to promote it.

If I have wrote with freedom, I consider I am writing to a friend, and that I am perfectly safe in opening myself to you.

I am, with great respect, Sir,
  Your most obedient humble servant,
    ANDREW OLIVER.

DEAR SIR :—The Commissioners of the Customs have met with every insult since their arrival at Boston, and at last have been obliged to seek protection on board his Majesty's ship Romney. Mr. Hallowell, the Comptroller of the Customs, who will have the honor to deliver you this letter, will inform you of many particulars; he is sent by the Board with their letters to government. Unless we have immediately two or three regiments, 'tis the opinion of all the friends to government, that Boston will be in open rebellion.

I have the honor to be, with the greatest respect and warmest regard,
  Dear Sir,
   Your most faithful and obliged servant,
    CHARLES PAXTON.

On board his Majesty's Ship Romney,
 Boston Harbor, June 20, 1768.

Boston, Dec. 12, 1768.

MY DEAR SIR:—I wrote you a few days ago, and did not then think of troubling you upon any private affair of mine, at least not so suddenly; but within this day or two, I have had a conversation with Mr. Oliver, Secre tary of the province, the design of which was my succeeding to the post he holds from the crown, upon the idea, that provision would be made for Governor Bernard, and the Lieutenant Governor would succeed to the chair, then the Secretary is desirous of being Lieutenant Governor, and if in any way three hundred pounds a year could be annexed to the appointment. You are sensible the appointment is in one department, and the grant in another; now the present Lieutenant Governor has an assignment of £200 a year upon the customs here; he has not received any thing from it as yet, and is doubtful if he shall; he has no doubt of its lapse to the crown, if he has the chair; if then by any interest, that sum could be assigned to Mr. Oliver as Lieutenant Governor, and if he should be allowed (as has been usual for all Lieutenant Governors) to hold the command of the castle, that would be another £100. This would complete the Secretary's views; and he thinks his public services, the injuries he has received in that service, and the favorable sentiments entertained of him by government, may lead him to these views, and he hopes for the interest of his friends. The place of Secretary is worth £300 a year, but is a provincial grant at present, so that it will not allow to be quartered on; and as I had views upon the place when I was in England, and went so far as to converse with several men of interest upon it, though I never had an opportunity to mention it to you after I recovered my illness. I hope you will allow me your influence, and by extending it at the Treasury, to facilitate the assignment of the £200 a year; it will be serving the Secretary, and it will very much oblige me. The Secretary is advanced in life, though much more so in health, which has been much impaired by the injuries he received, and he wishes to quit the more active scenes; he considers this as a kind of *otium cum dignitate*, and from merits one may think he has a claim to it. I will mention to you the gentlemen who are acquainted with my views, and whose favorable approbation I have had. Governor Pownall, Mr. John Pownall, and Dr. Franklin. My Lord Hillsborough is not unacquainted with it. I have, since I have been here, wrote Mr. Jackson upon the subject, and have by this vessel wrote Mr. Mauduit. I think my character stands fair. I have not been without application to public affairs, and have acquired some knowledge of our provincial affairs, and notwithstanding our many free conversations in England, I am considered here as on government side, for which I have been often traduced both publicly and privately, and very lately have had two or three slaps. The Governor and Lieutenant Governor are fully acquainted with the negotiation, and I meet their approbation; all is upon the idea the Governor is provided for, and there shall by any means be a vacancy of the Lieutenant Governor's place. I have gone so far as to say to some of my friends, that rather than not succeed I would agree to pay the Secretary £100 a year out of the office, to make up £300, provided he could obtain only the assignment of £200—but the other proposal would, to be sure, be most eligible. I scarce know any apology to make for troubling you upon the subject; the friendship you shewed me in London, and the favorable expressions you made use of to the Lieutenant Governor in my behalf, encourage me, besides a sort of egotism, which inclines men to think what they wish to be real.

I submit myself to the enquiries of any of my countrymen in England, but I should wish the matter may be secret till it is effected.

I am, with very great respect and regard, my dear Sir,
Your most obedient and most humble servant,
NATH. ROGERS.

REMARKS

IN DEFENCE OF THE FOREGOING LETTERS.

BY ISRAEL MAUDUIT.

THESE are the letters, upon which the Assembly have artfully been induced to pass their censures, and have founded an Address to remove his Majesty's Governor and Lieutenant Governor. Unable to point out a single action of the Governor's during his four years administration, they find themselves under a necessity of recurring to letters, written before the time, when either of these gentlemen were possessed of the offices which they now enjoy.

Upon the revival of them, I see strong proofs of Mr. Hutchinson's judgment and understanding, of his just notions of the interest of that country and of this, and of his fidelity and steady regard to the welfare of both: but am at a loss to find what there is in them, which can be a ground of blame; and much less warrant the very extraordinary censures, which have been passed on them. They are his private correspondence with the late Mr. Thomas Whately, a private Gentleman in London: a

Member of Parliament indeed, and one who has been Secretary to the Treasury: but who was then out of place; and far from being connected with Government, during the whole time while these letters were writing, was voting in opposition. Being neither of them in trade, their letters did not contain bills or invoices, but they turned upon subjects which Gentlemen naturally write about to each other: the occurrences of the time, and the several public matters, which were transacting in the places where each of them resided. The intelligences they contain may have come to hand something earlier than those by the common conveyance. But the facts themselves were, soon after, all known to every man in this country as well as that.

They give an account of a riot at Boston, upon the seizure of a smuggling vessel belonging to Mr. Hancock, a principal supporter of the party, and one of the Committee appointed to the management of the censure passed upon these letters; but of this riot we all of us in due time from our several correspondents, knew full as much as Mr. Whately did from his.*

The letters mention the combination at Boston against taking our goods: but is it a crime to write as news, what they wished to have told to all the world? and printed in their newspapers for that very purpose, in order to bully our Ministers, and frighten our Merchants and

---

* In this riot, Mr. Harrison, the Collector, an old Gentleman of an irreproachable character, and very respectable appearance, received a contusion in his breast by a brick-bat, which was thrown at him, under the ill-effects of which he languished for more than twelve months, and probably might have been trampled to death, if his son and others had not rescued him. This is what they called a Brush, or small disturbance with boys and negroes.

Manufacturers. They mention that upon the Governor's not judging it proper to call an Assembly at the will of the party leaders at Boston, these townsmen took upon themselves to write circular letters to all the towns and districts, to send one person each to Boston. And do we not all know that they did send such summons? and that this Mock Assembly did meet? and did they not desire that the world should know it, and publish their resolves for that purpose?

These letters mention the need there is of the government's supporting and encouraging the officers of the crown in the faithful discharge of their duty. And had not the House of Commons long before this determined the very same thing? and did they not address his Majesty, that he would so support and countenance them? They mention the common people's having been worked up into a frenzy, and their having talked of dying in defence of their liberties. And have they not been perpetually publishing threatenings of the same sort? and in all their papers sounding the trumpet of mutiny and sedition?

The letters say that many of rank above the vulgar, and some in public posts, had encouraged this frenzy. And do these censurers pretend to say they were not in such a state of confusion? Far from denying the truth of this account, the Committee of Council themselves acknowledge that "the state of things at this time was greatly disordered, but the greatness of this disorder they say arose from other causes; which they there enumerate." Whether they or Mr. Hutchinson were right in their judgment about the causes of these disorders is immaterial to the present argument. Both acknowledge that there were disorders. And had not Mr. Hutchinson as good a right to give his opinion about the causes of them to a private correspondent, as these gentlemen have openly to traduce the British Government, and to say that they were owing to them?

With the relation of these facts, the letters mention the writer's sentiments upon Government, and such other subjects as occur : sentiments which, as Mr. Hutchinson justly observes, contain nothing respecting the constitution of the colonies, more than what is contained in his public speeches to the Assembly. But whether they did or did not, will these sons of liberty, as they affect to call themselves, avow the position, that a Gentleman of Boston ought not to write his opinions to his friend in Loneon, unless those opinions do exactly coincide with theirs? I say nothing of the moderation and good temper which appears in all these letters ; for if they could have been still more temperate, yet, while Mr. Hutchinson stands in the way of the leaders of a faction, who can live by nothing but confusion, they would have equally condemned them. They wanted nothing more than to get some letters under the Governor's hand ; and whatever they were they would have condemned them in the same manner as they do these, and have found that the design of them was to overthrow the Constitution, and to introduce arbitrary power into the province. Thus they have treated their former Governors ; thus they have treated this ; and, if Mr. Hutchinson were to die, in three months time they would treat his successor in the same manner.

I might justly rest the matter here; and appeal to every impartial reader, whether if his own private correspondence should, by any act of fraud or perfidy, happen to be betrayed, he would not feel himself happy to find, that his letters contained as many things as these do, for his friends to commend, and so very few for the malice of his enemies to carp at. But as these men affect a mighty concern lest Mr. Whately should have shewed his letters to the King; and they might interrupt and "alienate the affections of our most gracious Sovereign King George the Third, from his loyal and affectionate province; and destroy the harmony and good-will between Great Britain and that colony, which every friend to either would wish to establish:" and as the generality of people here, misled by false representations and feigned letters in newspapers, are but too apt to believe them, this makes it necessary to take off the mask of hypocrisy, and to exhibit them in their own proper features. When the reader will himself see, that all these fearful apprehensions of his Majesty's displeasure, and all these professed desires of harmony between Great Britain and the Colony, are mere mockery and insult; and that they really mean the direct contrary.

See, reader, the true standard of their loyalty, extracted from the Journals of the last House of Representatives. The party had it not in their power to make a declaratory Act of Assembly, because they knew that the Governor would not pass it: but they passed the following declaratory resolutions :

Mercurii, 3 *die Martii*, A. D. 1773.

"The House, according to order, entered into the consideration of the report of the Committee appointed to consider his Excellency's message relative to the salaries

REMARKS IN DEFENCE OF THE FOREGOING LETTERS. 57

of the Justices of the Superior Court; and thereupon the following resolves were passed :

"*Whereas*, by an act of the British Parliament, made and passed in the sixth year of his present Majesty's reign, it is declared, That the King, Lords, and Commons in Parliament assembled have, ever had, and of right ought to have, full power and authority to make laws and statutes of sufficient force and validity, to bind the colonies and people of America, subjects of the Crown of Great Britain, in all cases whatever; and afterwards the same Parliament made and passed an act for levying duties in America, with the express purpose of raising a revenue, and to enable his Majesty to appropriate the same for the necessary charges of the administration of justice, and the support of civil government in such colonies where it shall be judged necessary, and towards further defraying the expenses of defending, protecting, and securing said dominions. And his Majesty has been pleased, by virtue of the same last-mentioned act, to appropriate a part of the revenue thus raised against the consent of the people, in providing for the support of the Governor of the province; and from his Excellency's message of the 4th of February we cannot but conclude, that provision is made for the support of the Judges of the Superior Court of Judicature, independent of the grants and acts of the General Assembly, contrary to the invariable usage of this province :" therefore,

"*Resolved*, That the admitting any authority to make laws binding on the people of this province in all cases whatsoever, saving the General Court or Assembly, is inconsistent with the spirit of our free constitution, and is repugnant to one of the most essential clauses in our charter, whereby the inhabitants are entitled to all the liberties of free and natural born subjects, to all intents, constructions, and purposes whatsoever, as if they had been born within the realm of England. It reduces the people to the absolute will and disposal of a Legislature, in which they can have no voice, and who may make it their interest to oppress and enslave them.

"*Resolved*, That by the Royal Charter aforesaid, 'the General Court or Assembly hath full power and authority to impose and levy proportionable and reasonable assessments, rates, and taxes, upon the estates and persons of all and every the proprietors and inhabitants of the province, to be issued and disposed of by warrant, under the hand of the Governor, with the advice and consent of the Council, for his Majesty's service in the necessary defence and support of the government of the province, and the protection and preservation of the inhabitants there, according to such acts as are or shall be in force within the province.' And the making provision for the support of the Governor and the Judges otherwise than by the grants and acts of the General Court or Assembly, is a violent breach of the aforesaid most important clause in the charter: the support of government, in which their support is included, being one of the principal purposes for which the clause was inserted.

"*Whereas* the independence as well as the uprightness of the Judges of the land is essential to the impartial administration of justice, and one of the best securities of the rights, liberties, and properties of the people,

"*Resolved*, therefore, That the making the Judges of the land independent of the grants of the people, and altogether dependent on the crown, as they will be, if while they thus hold their commissions during pleasure, they accept of salaries from the crown, is unconstitutional and destructive of that security, which every good member of civil society has a just right to be assured of, under the due execution of the laws, and is directly the reverse of the constitution and appointment of the Judges in Great Britain.

"*Resolved*, That the dependence of the Judges of the land on the crown for their support, tends at all times, especially while they hold their commissions during pleasure, to the subversion of justice and equity, and to introduce oppression and despotic power.

"*Resolved*, As the opinion of this House, that while the Justices of the Superior Court hold their commissions during pleasure, any one of them who shall accept of, and depend upon the pleasure of the crown for his support, independent of the grants and acts of the General Assembly, will discover to the world, that he has not a due sense of 'the importance of an impartial administration of justice, that he is an enemy to the constitution, and has it in his heart to promote the establishment of an arbitrary government in the province.'"

Reader, after the perusal of these resolutions, what are all the things said of these men in Mr. Hutchinson's letters, compared with what they here say of themselves? Or what is there in his mentioning some particular instances of their not paying a due obedience to the authority of government, compared with this open disavowal of the whole? Yet the Committee, which drew up these resolutions, consisted chiefly of the same individual men, with the Committee, which drew up the censure on these letters. And indeed they are the same set of men, whose names appear in all Committees of this sort. These are the men, who, in order to give a plausible color to their censures, can transform themselves into the appearance of the most meek and submissive of all his Majesty's subjects, and affect to be greatly alarmed at these private letters, and to believe that "they had a natural and efficacious tendency to interrupt and alienate the affections of our Most Gracious Sovereign, King George the Third, from this his loyal and affectionate province; to destroy that harmony and good will between Great Britain and this colony, which every friend to either would wish to establish; and to excite the resentment of the British Administration against this province, &c."

At that very time, when they knew that they had been flying in the face of his Majesty, setting acts of parliament at defiance, and passing the most seditious resolutions against the dignity of the British nation, and the supreme authority of the empire; at that very time these tender-minded loyalists are most piteously concerned about some private letters, lest they should interrupt and alienate the affections of their Most Gracious Sovereign King George the Third: letters which set them in a light of innocence, compared with the mutinous and insolent portrait, which they have here drawn of themselves.

After having in their public votes spurned at the King's orders, assumed to themselves the control of his Courts of Justice, and proscribed the King's Judges as enemies to the constitution, and promoters of arbitrary government, if they obey the King's order, founded on an act of parliament, and receive the King's salaries, they then call themselves his most loyal and affectionate subjects.

They openly recite a solemn act of the British legislature, and make a counter declaration of their own in direct opposition to it; and then pretend to be mightily afraid, lest these letters to Mr. Whately should destroy the harmony and good-will between Great Britain and the colony.

But not content with professing their great concern to preserve the good-will of the British nation, and to appear to his Majesty as his most affectionate subjects, they are anxious even about the good opinion of his Ministers; and are grievously concerned, lest these letters should *excite the resentment of the British Administration.* Reader, these very men, Adams, Hancock, &c., who, in the form of a Committee of Correspondence for the town of Boston, have been inflaming all the towns in the province against the King's government; who, in the form of a Committee of Assembly, drew up these resolutions, and these censures; these very men, in a message to the Governor, 12th February, 1773, express themselves in the following terms: "We are more and more convinced, that it has been the design of the Administration, totally to subvert the constitution, and to introduce arbitrary government into this province." Doubtless, the King's servants ought, every man of them, to join in advising his Majesty to dismiss his Governor and Lieutenant Governor, who could suppose any thing ill of men who stood so much in awe of *their resentment?*

There is one remark more, which cannot have escaped the reader. One of the chief passages objected to by these censurers, is that where Mr. Hutchinson says: "If no measures shall have been taken to secure this dependence, or nothing more than some declaratory acts or resolves, it is all over with us." Can there possibly be required a stronger proof of the truth of this observation about the inefficacy of our declaratory act, than the counter declaration which we have now seen? yet, after having themselves verified the prediction, they would have his Majesty turn out his Governor for having made it.

Reader, there are but too many men to be found, who, after doing a bad thing, will be false enough to charge it upon others. There are also other instances of men, who having done a wrong thing, will affect to consider as the highest affront, they being told that they have done it. But for men first to do a thing, then to avow it, and publish to the world that they have done it, and after all this to censure it as a crime in their Governor to suppose them capable of doing it,—this is a degree of effrontery suited only to the complexion of a Boston Committee-man.

There are a few other remarks which it may be of use to make upon these letters.

The only exceptionable expression in Mr. Hutchinson's letters, is that in which he says, *there must be an abridgment of what are called English Liberties*. And this appears so, only from our not being apprized of the meaning of it. An English reader naturally concludes, that by *English Liberties* is meant our being governed, not by arbitrary will, but only by Acts of Parliament. In the Boston new dialect the import of this phrase is just the contrary; and what *they* call *English Liberties*, is the *not* being governed by Acts of Parliament. The reader need only look into their votes and public proceedings, to be convinced that this is the true and avowed sense in which they understand it. In the Charter of the Massachusetts colony, King William, in the words of their old Charter, says: "And farther our will and pleasure is, and we do hereby for us, our heirs, and successors, grant, establish, and ordain, That all and every of the subjects of us, our heirs, and successors, which shall go to and inhabit within our said province and territory, and every of their children, which shall happen to be born there, or on the seas in going thither, or returning from thence, shall have and enjoy all liberties and immunities of free and natural subjects, *within any of the dominions of us, our heirs, and successors*, to all intents, constructions, and purposes whatsoever, as if they and every of them were born within this our realm of England." From King William's reign to this, no one ever had the least doubt about the meaning of this clause; and the New Englanders have ever enjoyed the full benefit of it, by their being treated in all parts of the King's dominions, wherever they came, not as aliens, but as denisons, and enjoying all the liberties and immunities of free and natural born subjects. This, I say, has invariably hitherto been understood to be the meaning of this paragraph. But within these few years, the leaders of the faction at Boston have been instructed to put a quite new interpretation upon these words, and to say: The people of England have a right to choose Representatives for themselves, and are governed only by Acts of Parliament; the charter says, that we shall enjoy all liberties and immunities of free and natural subjects within any of the King's dominions; therefore we too have as good a right, as the people of England have, to choose our own Representatives, and to be governed only by the laws made by our own Assembly; and the Parliament of England have nothing to do with us. We, as well as the inhabitants of England, by our charter are entitled to English liberties, and therefore we will make laws for ourselves; and no legislature of Great Britain has any right to control us.

A subordinate power of legislation, for the well ordering the several provinces and corporations, and for the making laws for their own good government among themselves, *that* is a power which we can well understand; and accordingly in the Massachusetts Charter, as well as in most other Charters, there is an express clause, giving them this legislative power, and limiting the extent of it; that its laws shall not be repugnant or contrary to the laws of the realm, or as the next paragraph says, repugnant to the laws and statutes of this our realm. But these Bostoners passing over this, and all the other clauses in their Charter, which provide for their welfare and good government, while they continue in the province, have most unfortunately chosen to build their high claim of independence upon that single clause which grants them nothing while they are *in* the province, but only provides for their good reception *in all parts of the King's dominions*, when they go *out* of it.

In opposition to this wild and futile claim of independence, Mr. Hutchinson insists, " that from King William's days to these, the oldest man living never heard of this interpretation. That never before these days was a doubt made of the supreme authority of Parliament over every part of the empire. That in every government there must be somewhere a supreme uncontrolable power, an absolute authority to decide and determine. That two such powers cannot co-exist, but necessarily will make two distinct states."

Whether it be right or not, that the empire should be split into a number of separate and independent governments, which shall each of them be at liberty to take their own course, and make laws according to their own liking, without being subject to any control from that supreme legislature, which has hitherto been thought to have the care of the whole, and whose duty it is to see that no part of the empire suffer any detriment, that is an argument which I leave to the determination of a superior authority.

Whether it be a justifiable procedure to foster and encourage this froward humor in the Colonists, and to support them in these pretensions of independence, till we have nursed up their discontents into mutiny and rebellion,—whether, I say, it be a justifiable thing to do this, for the single purpose of distressing or oversetting a ministry, that I leave to the discretion of our party leaders.

All that I have to observe is this : That if by English liberties and immunities be meant a right given to a set of subjects, wherever they go, to erect a legislature of their own, and then to say that they will be governed by that only, and that the Parliament has nothing to do with them; if, immediately after King James had been expelled for attempting to suspend *a very few* Acts of Parliament, it can be supposed, that King William meant to assume a power to suspend them *all*,—we may then allow, that the people of Boston have a right to vote these to be English liberties.

But if the British empire be but one empire, and we do not wish to see it crumble to pieces, and break it into as many separate governments, as are the provinces, counties, and corporations contained in it: we must then be convinced, that a grant of English liberties and immunities does not mean a right given to every province or corporation of the empire, to separate itself from the rest of the British dominions, and to form to itself a legislature of its own, which shall be uncontrolable by Parliament.

Or, if the people of Massachusetts Bay will persist in the use of this phrase, and will say, that this ought to be called English liberties; we must then say, as Mr. Hutchinson does, that the British empire is but one, and that to preserve that unity, there must be an abridgment of what are (thus absurdly) called *English liberties.*

PROCEEDINGS ON THE ADDRESS

OF THE

ASSEMBLY OF MASSACHUSETTS BAY,

TO REMOVE

HIS MAJESTY'S GOVERNOR AND LIEUTENANT GOVERNOR.

To the Right Hon. the Earl of DARTMOUTH.
(COPY.)
London, August 21, 1773.

MY LORD :—I have just received from the House of Representatives of the Massachusetts Bay, their Address to the King, which I now enclose, and send to your Lordship with my humble request in their behalf, that you would be pleased to present it to his Majesty the first convenient opportunity.

I have the pleasure of hearing from that province by my late letters, that a sincere disposition prevails in the people there to be on good terms with the Mother Country; that the Assembly have declared their desire only to be put into the situation they were in before the stamp act; they aim at no novelties. And it is said, that having lately discovered, as they think, the authors of their grievances to be some of their own people, their resentment against Britain is thence much abated.

This good disposition of theirs (will your Lordship permit me to say?) may be cultivated by a favorable answer to this Address, which I therefore hope your goodness will endeavor to obtain.

With the greatest respect,
I have the Honor to be, my Lord, &c.,
B. FRANKLIN,
Agent for the House of Representatives.

To the Clerk of the Council in waiting.
(COPY.)
Whitehall, Dec. 3, 1773.

SIR:—The Agent for the House of Representatives of the Province of the Massachusetts Bay, having delivered to Lord Dartmouth an Address of that House to the King, signed by their Speaker, complaining of the conduct of the Governor and Lieutenant Governor of that province, in respect to certain private letters written by them to their correspondents in England, and praying that they may be removed from their posts in that government; his Lordship hath presented the said Address to his Majesty; and his Majesty having signified his pleasure, that the said Address should be laid before his Majesty in his Privy Council, I am directed by Lord Dartmouth to transmit the same accordingly, together with a copy of the Agent's letter to his Lordship accompanying the said Address.

I am, Sir,
Your most obedient humble servant,
(Signed.) J. POWNALL.

To the KING's Most Excellent Majesty.

MOST GRACIOUS SOVEREIGN :—We, your Majesty's loyal subjects, the Representatives of your ancient Colony of the Massachusetts Bay, in General Court legally assembled, by virtue of your Majesty's writ, under the hand and seal of the Governor, beg leave to lay this our humble Petition before your Majesty.

Nothing but the sense of the duty we owe to our Sovereign, and the obligation we are under to consult the peace and safety of the Province, could induce us to remonstrate to your Majesty the Mal-Conduct of persons who have heretofore had the confidence and esteem of this people; and whom your Majesty has been pleased, from the purest motives of rendering your subjects happy, to advance to the highest places of trust and authority in the Province.

Your Majesty's humble petitioners, with the deepest concern and anxiety, have seen the discords and animosities which have too long subsisted between your subjects of the Parent State and those of the American Colonies. And we have trembled with apprehensions that the consequences, naturally arising therefrom, would at length prove fatal to both Countries.

Permit us humbly to suggest to your Majesty, that your subjects here have been inclined to believe, that the grievances which they have suffered, and still continue to suffer, have been occasioned by your Majesty's ministers and principal servants being, unfortunately for us, misinformed in certain facts of very interesting importance to us. It is for this reason that former Assemblies have from time to time prepared a true state of facts to be laid before your Majesty, but their humble remonstrances and petitions, it is presumed, have by some means been prevented from reaching your Royal hand.

Your Majesty's petitioners have very lately had before them certain papers, from which they humbly conceive, it is most reasonable to suppose, that there has long been a conspiracy of evil men in this province, who have contemplated measures and formed a plan to advance themselves to power, and raise their own fortunes, by means destructive of the charter of the province, at the expense of the quiet of the nation, and to the annihilating of the rights and liberties of the American colonies.

And we do, with all due submission to your Majesty, beg leave particularly to complain of the conduct of his Excellency, Thomas Hutchinson, Esquire, Governor, and the Honorable Andrew Oliver, Esquire, Lieutenant Governor, of this your Majesty's province, as having a natural and efficacious tendency to interrupt and alienate the affections of your Majesty, our Rightful Sovereign, from this your Loyal Province, to destroy that harmony and good-will between Great Britain and this Colony, which every honest subject would strive to establish, to excite the resentment of the British Administration against this province, to defeat the endeavors of our agents and friends to serve us by a fair representation of our state of facts, to prevent our humble and repeated petitions from reaching the ear of your Majesty, or having their desired effect. And finally, that the said Thomas Hutchinson and Andrew Oliver have been among the chief instruments in introducing a fleet and an army into this province, to establish and perpetuate their plans; whereby they have been not only greatly instrumental of disturbing the peace and harmony of the government, and causing unnatural and hateful discords and animosities between the several parts of your Majesty's extensive dominions, but are justly chargeable with all that corruption of morals and all that confusion, misery, and bloodshed, which have been the natural effects of posting an army in a populous town.

Wherefore we most humbly pray that your Majesty would be pleased to remove from their posts in this government, the said Thomas Hutchinson, Esquire, and Andrew Oliver, Esquire, who have, by their above-mentioned conduct and otherwise, rendered themselves justly obnoxious to your loving subjects, and entirely lost their confidence; and place such good and faithful men in their stead as your Majesty in your great wisdom shall think fit.

In the name and by order of the House of Representatives,

THO. CUSHING,
Speaker.

TO THE LORDS' COMMITTEE OF HIS MAJESTY'S PRIVY COUNCIL, FOR PLANTATION AFFAIRS.

The Petition of Israel Mauduit, humbly showeth unto your Lordships:

That having been informed that an Address in the name of the House of Representatives of his Majesty's Colony of Massachusetts Bay, has been presented to his Majesty, by Benjamin Franklin, Esq., praying the removal of his Majesty's Governor and Lieutenant Governor, which is appointed to be taken into consideration on Tuesday next. Your petitioner, on the behalf of the said Governor and Lieutenant Governor, humbly prays, that he may be heard by counsel in relation to the same, before your Lordships shall make any report on the said Address.

ISRAEL MAUDUIT.

Clemens Lane, Jan. 10, 1774.

To the Printer of the Public Advertiser.

SIR:—Finding that two gentlemen have been unfortunately engaged in a duel, about a transaction and its circumstances, of which both of them are totally ignorant and innocent, I think it incumbent on me to declare (for the prevention of farther mischief, as far as such a declaration may contribute to prevent it) that I alone am the person who obtained and transmitted to Boston the letters in question. Mr. W. could not communicate them, because they were never in his possession; and for the same reason, they could not be taken from him by Mr. T. They were not of the nature of private letters between friends. They were written by public officers to persons in public station, on public affairs, and intended to procure public measures; they were therefore handed to other public persons who might be influenced by them to produce those measures. Their tendency was to incense the mother country against her colonies, and, by the steps recommended, to widen the breach which they effected. The chief caution expressed with regard to privacy, was, to keep their contents from the Colony

Agents, who, the writers apprehended, might return them, or copies of them, to America. That apprehension was, it seems, well founded; for the first agent who laid his hands on them, thought it his duty to transmit them to his constituents.

B. FRANKLIN,

Agent for the House of Representatives of Massachusetts Bay. Craven Street, Dec. 25, 1773.

AT THE COUNCIL CHAMBER, Jan. 11, 1774.

Present, Lord President, Secretaries of State, and many other Lords.

DR. FRANKLIN and MR. BOLLAN,
MR. MAUDUIT and MR. WEDDERBURN.

Dr. Franklin's Letter, and the Address, Mr. Pownal's Letter, and Mr. Mauduit's Petition, were read.

Mr. Wedderburn.—The Address mentions certain papers. I would wish to be informed what are those papers.

Dr. Franklin.—They are the letters of Mr. Hutchinson and Mr. Oliver.

Court.—Have you brought them?

Dr Franklin.—No; but here are attested copies.

Court.—Do you not mean to found a charge upon them? If you do, you must produce the letters.

Dr. Franklin.—These copies are attested by several gentlemen at Boston, and a Notary Public.

Mr. Wedderburn.—My Lords, we shall not take advantage of any imperfection in the proof. We admit that the letters are Mr. Hutchinson's and Mr. Oliver's hand writing, reserving to ourselves the right of inquiring how they were obtained.

Dr. Franklin.—I did not expect that counsel would have been employed on this occasion.

Court.—Had you not notice sent you of Mr. Mauduit's having petitioned to be heard by counsel on behalf of the Governor and Lieutenant Governor?

Dr. Franklin.—I did receive such notice, but I thought that this had been a matter of politics and not of law, and have not brought any counsel.

Court.—Where a charge is brought, the parties have a right to be heard by counsel or not, as they choose.

Mr. Mauduit.—My Lords, I am not a native of that country, as these gentlemen are. I well know Dr. Franklin's abilities, and wish to put the defence of my friends more upon a parity with the attack; he will not therefore wonder that I choose to appear before your Lordships with the assistance of counsel. My friends, in their letters to me, have desired (if any proceedings, as they say, should be had upon this Address) that they may have a hearing in their own justification, that their innocence may be fully cleared, and their honor vindicated; and have made provision accordingly. I do not think myself at liberty, therefore, to give up the assistance of my counsel, in defending them against this unjust accusation.

Court.—Dr. Franklin may have the assistance of counsel, or go on without it, as he shall choose.

Dr. Franklin.—I desire to have counsel.

Court.—What time shall you want?

Dr. Franklin.—Three weeks.

Ordered, That the further proceedings be on Saturday, 29th instant.

The substance of that part of Mr. Wedderburn's Speech which related to the obtaining and sending away Mr. Whately's Letters.

Counsel for the Assembly.
MR. DUNNING, MR. JOHN LEE.

Counsel for the Governor and Lieutenant Governor.
MR. WEDDERBURN.

AT THE COUNCIL CHAMBER,
Saturday, Jan. 29, 1774.

Present, Lord President and thirty-five Lords.

MR. WEDDERBURN.

MY LORDS:—The case which now comes before your Lordships is justly entitled to all that attention, which, from the presence of so great a number of Lords, and of so large an audience, it appears to have excited. It is a question of no less magnitude, than whether the Crown shall ever have it in its power to employ a faithful and steady servant in the administration of a Colony.

In the appointment of Mr. Hutchinson, his Majesty's choice followed the wishes of his people; and no other man could have been named, in whom so many favorable circumstances concurred to recommend him.

A native of the country, whose ancestors were among

its first settlers. A gentleman, who had for many years presided in their law courts; of tried integrity, of confessed abilities; and who had long employed those abilities, in the study of their history and original constitution.

My Lords, if such a man, without their attempting to allege one single act of misconduct, during the four years in which he has been Governor, is to be borne down by the mere surmises of this Address, it must then become a case of still greater magnitude, and ever be a matter of doubt, whether the Colony shall henceforward pay respect to any authority derived from this country.

A charge of some sort, however, is now preferred against these gentlemen by this Address; and the prayer of it is, that his Majesty would punish them by a disgraceful removal.

If they shall appear to have either betrayed the rights of the Crown, or to have invaded the rights of the people, your Lordships doubtless will then advise his Majesty no longer to trust his authority with those who have abused it.

But if no crime is objected to them, no act of misconduct proved, your Lordships will then do the justice to their characters, which every innocent man has a right to expect, and grant them that protection and encouragement, which is due to officers in their station.

My Lords, this is not the place to give any opinion about our public transactions relating to the Colonies, and I shall carefully avoid it. But the whole foundation of this Address rests upon events of five and six years standing; and this makes it necessary to take up the history of them from their first original.

In the beginning of the year 1764, * * *
* * * * * * * * * *

My Lords, after having gone through the history of this people, for the last ten years, and shown what has been the behaviour of Mr. Hutchinson in all these occurrences, and the very laudable and friendly part he acted on every occasion for the good of the colony; I now come to consider the argument upon that footing, on which my learned friends have chosen to place it.

They have read to your Lordships the Assembly's address; they have read the letters; and they have read the censures passed on them: and, after praying the removal of his Majesty's Governor and Lieutenant Governor, they now tell your Lordships: There is no cause to try—there is no charge—there are no accusers—there are no proofs. They say that the Governor and Lieutenant Governor are disliked by the Assembly, and they ought to be dismissed, because they have lost the confidence *of those* who complain against them.

My Lords, this is so very extraordinary a proceeding, that 1 know of no precedent, except one: but that, I confess, according to the Roman poet's report, is a case in point:

> Nunquam, si quid mihi credis, amavi
> Hunc hominem. Sed quo cecidit sub crimine?—Quisnam
> Delator—Quibus Indicibus?—Quo Teste probavit—
> Nil horum—Verbosa et grandis epistola venit
> A Capreis—Bene habet: nil plus interrogo.

My Lords, the only purport of this important Address is, that the Governor and Lieutenant Governor have lost the confidence of the people, upon account of some papers, which they have voted to be unfriendly to them, and *that they have been amongst the chief instruments in introducing a fleet and army into the province.* Your Lordships have heard the letters read, and are the best judges of their tendency. I can appeal to your Lordships, that it was not these letters, but their own ill conduct, which made it necessary to order the four regiments. In point of time it was impossible : for in Mr. Hutchinson's very first letter, it appears, that they had an expectation of troops. And they arrived in three months after. I could appeal too to their own knowledge: for the printed collection of Sir Francis Bernard's and General Gage's, &c., letters were before them, which indisputably show the direct contrary.

But as my learned friends have not attempted to point out the demerits of these letters, I need not enter into the defence of them. To call them only innocent letters, would be greatly to depreciate them. They contain the strongest proofs of Mr. Hutchinson's good sense, his great moderation, and his sincere regard to the welfare of that his native province. Yet, for these it is, that they tell us he has lost the confidence of the people.

My Lords, there cannot be a more striking instance of the force of truth, than what the Committee, who drew up these papers, exemplify in their conduct. In their second resolution, they acknowledge the high character, in which Mr. Hutchinson stands, upon account of his *eminent abilities.* In the very outset of their address, they acknowledge the good *use* which he had made of those abilities : for he could not have enjoyed their confidence, as they say he heretofore did, if he had made a bad one. They acknowledge that this confidence subsisted, at least, till the time of his being made Governor.

Else they could not express their thankfulness to his Majesty as they do, and applaud the appointment of him, *as proceeding from the purest motives of rendering his subjects happy.*

In the height of their ill-will, therefore, to Mr. Hutchinson, truth looks his enemies full in the face, and extorts from them a confession of his merit, even in the very act of accusing him.

But, whatever be the censures which the Assembly may have been induced to pass on him, I will now give your Lordships a proof of his enjoying the people's confidence, to the very time of the arrival of these letters.

Every one knows that there are few subjects in which the people of the colonies have more eagerly interested themselves, than in settling the boundary lines between the several provinces. Some of your Lordships may remember the long hearings which have been held at this Board upon these disputes. Of late, they have taken upon *themselves* to fix the limits of the King's charters. An agreement was made between the two Assemblies of New York and Massachusetts Bay, that they should each appoint their Commissaries, to meet and settle the boundary line between the two provinces. Both of them no doubt looked out for the best men they had for that purpose. But the people of Massachusetts Bay, after they had chosen their Commissaries, still thought that they could more securely trust their interests in their hands, if Mr. Hutchinson would go along with them. To him they had been used to look, as the man who best knew the history of their first settlements; him they considered as the ablest defender of the province's rights: and had ever found in him the most zealous affection for their welfare. The party leaders perhaps might have been content to lose to the province any number of acres or a few townships, rather than owe to Mr. Hutchinson the preservation of them. But they did not dare to set their faces against the general sense of the people. The Governor was therefore requested to go with the Commissaries. He did so, and settled for them a much better line than they had ever expected. And the New York and their own Commissaries, both of them acknowledged that the advantage gained to the province, was chiefly owing to the superior knowledge and abilities of Mr. Hutchinson.

Thus far, then, the Governor's character stands fair and unimpeached. Whatever, therefore, be the foundation of this Address for his removal, it must be something done by him, or known of him, since his return from this service just before the arrival of these letters. Your Lordships will observe that his enemies don't attempt to point out a single action, during the four years in which he has been Governor, as a subject of complaint. The whole of this Address rests upon the foundation of these letters, written before the time when either of these gentlemen were possessed of the offices, from which the Assembly now ask their removal. They owe therefore all the ill-will which has been raised against them, and the loss of that confidence which the Assembly themselves acknowledge they had heretofore enjoyed, to Dr. Franklin's good office in sending back these letters to Boston. Dr. Franklin therefore stands in the light of the first mover and prime conductor of this whole contrivance against his Majesty's two Governors; and having by the help of his special confidents and party leaders, first made the Assembly *his*

Agents in carrying on his own secret designs, he now appears before your Lordships to give the finishing stroke to the work of his own hands.

How these letters came into the possession of any one but the right owners, is still a mystery for Dr. Franklin to explain. They who know the affectionate regard which the Whatelys had for each other, and the tender concern they felt for the honor of their brother's memory, as well as their own, can witness the distresses which this occasioned. My Lords, the late Mr. Whately was most scrupulously cautious about his letters. We lived for many years in the strictest intimacy; and in all those years I never saw a single letter written to him. These letters, I believe, were in his custody at his death. And I as firmly believe, that without fraud, they could not have been got out of the custody of the person whose hands they fell into. His brothers little wanted this additional aggravation to the loss of him. Called upon by their correspondents at Boston; anxious for vindicating their brother's honor and their own, they enquired; gave to the parties aggrieved all the information in their power; but never accused.

Your Lordships know the train of mischiefs which followed. But wherein had my late worthy friend or his family offended Dr. Franklin, that he should first do so great an injury to the memory of the dead brother, by secreting and sending away his letters; and then, conscious of what he had done, should keep himself concealed, till he had nearly, very nearly, occasioned the murder of the other.

After the mischiefs of this concealment had been left for five months to have their full operation, at length comes out a letter, which it is impossible to read without horror; expressive of the coolest and most deliberate malevolence. My Lords, what poetic fiction only had penned for the *breast* of a cruel African, Dr. Franklin has realized, and transcribed from his *own*. His too is the language of a Zanga:

" Know then 'twas ——— I.

" I forged the letter—I disposed the picture—

" I hated, I despised, and I destroy."

What are the motives he assigns for this conduct, I shall now more deliberately consider.

My Lords, if there be any thing held sacred in the intercourse of mankind, it is their private letters of friendship. If there can be any such private letters, those which passed between the late Mr. Whately and Mr. Oliver are such. The friendship between the two families is of thirty years' standing,—during all that time there has been kept up an intercourse of letters; first with Mr. Whately, the father, and then with the late Mr. Thomas Whately, the son. In the course of this friendship, a variety of good offices have passed between the two families: one of these fell within the period of these letters. Upon Mr. Oliver's daughter's coming to England with her husband upon business, they were received at Nonsuch by Mrs. Whately and her sons, as the son and daughter of their old friend and correspondent. And accordingly your Lordships will find, that one part of these letters is to return thanks for the civilities shown to Mr. and Mrs. Spooner at Nonsuch.

These are the letters which Dr. Franklin treats as public letters, and has thought proper to secrete them for his own private purpose. How he got at them, or in whose hands they were at the time of Mr. Whately's death, the Doctor has not yet thought proper to tell us. Till he do, he wittingly leaves the world at liberty to conjecture about them as they please, and to reason upon those conjectures. But let the letters have been lodged where they may, from the hour of Mr. Thomas Whately's death, they became the property of his brother and of the Whately family. Dr. Franklin could not but know this, and that no one had a right to dispose of them but they only. Other receivers of goods dishonorably come by, may plead as a pretence for keeping them, that they don't know who are the proprietors. In this case there was not the common excuse of ignorance; the Doctor knew whose they were, and yet did not restore them to the right owner. This property is as sacred and as precious to gentlemen of integrity, as their family plate or jewels are. And no man who knows the Whatelys will doubt but that they would much sooner have chosen, that any person should have taken their plate, and sent it to Holland for his avarice, than that he should have secreted the letters of their friends, their brother's friend, and their father's friend, and sent them away to Boston, to gratify an enemy's malice.

The reasons assigned for this, are as extraordinary as the transaction itself is: They are public letters, to public persons, on public affairs, and intended to produce public measures. This, my Lords, is the first; and the next reason assigned for publishing them is, because the writers desire that the contents of them should be kept secret.

If these are public letters, I know not what can be reckoned private. If a letter whose first business is to return thanks to an old lady of seventy, for her civilities at Nonsuch, be not a private letter, it will be necessary that every man should be particularly careful of his papers; for, after this, there never can be wanting a pretence for making them public.*

But says the Doctor, "*They were written by public officers.*" Can then a man in a public station have no private friends, and write no private letters? Will Dr. Franklin avow the principle, that he has a right to make all private letters of your Lordships his own, and to apply them to such uses as will best answer the purposes of party malevolence? Whatever may have been the confidence heretofore placed in him, such a declaration will not surely contribute to increase it.

But they were written *to persons in public stations.* Just the contrary to this appears to have been the case. Dr. Franklin is too well acquainted with our history not to know that Mr. Whately, during both these years, and for two years before and after, was only a private Member of Parliament; and, as Mr. Oliver justly observes in a letter of his, *They at Boston could not be supposed to apply to him as having an interest with the Ministers, when they knew that he was all that time voting in opposition to them.*

Does then the Doctor mean, that his being a Member of Parliament placed him in a public station? And will he then avow, that a gentleman's being in Parliament is ground sufficient for *him* to make his letters lawful plunder, and to send them to his enemies?

But *they were written on public affairs.* A very grievous

---

* The reader will be pleased to observe, that the question here is not whether they be good letters or bad ones, but whether they are public letters or private.

offence! But it is a crime of which probably we all of us have been guilty, and ought not surely, for that only, to forfeit the common rights of humanity.

But *they were intended to procure public measures.* And does not every man, who writes in confidence to his friend upon political subjects, lament any thing which he thinks to be wrong, and wish to have it amended? And is this a crime of so heinous a nature, as to put Mr. Whately's friends out of the common protection, and to give to Dr. Franklin a right to hang them up to party rage, and to expose them, for what he knew, to the danger of having their houses a second time pulled down by popular fury?

But *the writers of them desired secresy.* True, they did so. And what man is there, who, when he is writing in confidence, does not wish for the same thing? Does not every man say things to a friend, which he would not choose to have published to other people, and much less to his enemies? Would letters of friendship *be* letters of friendship, if they contained nothing but such indifferent things as might be said to all the world?

If this is the case at all times with the confidential intercourse of friends, in times of party violence, there must be a thousand things said in letters, which, though innocent in themselves, either by rival malice or party prejudice, may be turned to a very different construction. These letters themselves have been distorted in this manner; and some expressions in them cannot possibly be understood, without knowing the correspondent letters to which they refer. And when a factious party had got possession of the town meetings, and led the Assembly into what resolutions they pleased, and were watching for any pretence to abuse and insult their Governors, is it at all to be wondered, that they did not wish to have the contents of their letters told to their enemies?

When we read in these letters such passages as these: "If there be no necessity for it, I think it would be best it should not be known that this intelligence comes from me." Or this: "I have wrote with freedom, in confidence of my name's not being used on the occasion. For though I have wrote nothing but what, in my conscience, I think an American may, upon just principles, advance, and what a servant of the crown ought, upon all proper occasions, to suggest; yet the many prejudices I have to combat with, may render it unfit it should be made public." Or this of Mr. Hutchinson's: "I must beg the favor of you to keep secret every thing I write, until we are in a more settled state; for the party here, either by their Agent, or by some of their emissaries in London, have sent them every report or rumor of the *contents* of letters wrote from hence. I hope we shall see better times both here and in England." Or this again of Mr. Oliver's: "*I have wrote with freedom; I consider I am writing to a friend; and that I am perfectly safe in opening myself to you.*" Upon reading these passages, which are all there are of this kind, a man whose heart was cast in the common mould of humanity, would have been apt to say: These are letters irregularly obtained; the writers desire that every thing they write should be kept secret; they belong to Mr. Whately, who never injured *me*; I will therefore return them to the right owner. Dr. Franklin's reasoning is of a very different cast. After having just before told us: These are public letters, sent to public persons, designed for public purposes, and *therefore* I have a right to betray them; he now says, These are letters which the writers desire may be kept secret, and therefore I will send them to their enemies. Prepared on both sides for his rival's overthrow, he makes that an argument for doing him hurt, which any other man would consider as a principal aggravation of the injustice of it.

But, if the desiring secresy be the proof, and the measure of guilt, what then are we to think of Dr. Franklin's case; whose whole conduct in this affair has been secret and mysterious; and who, through the whole course of it, has discovered the utmost solicitude to keep it so? My Lords, my accounts say, that when these letters were sent over to Boston, so very desirous was Dr. Franklin of secresy, that he did not choose to set his name to the letter which accompanied them. This anonymous letter expressly ordered, that it should be shown to none but to a junto of six persons. If the Doctor choose it, I will name the six. The direction of every letter was erased, and strict orders were given that they should be carefully returned again to London. The manner in which they were brought into the Assembly, all showed the most earnest desire of concealment. Under these mysterious circumstances have the Assembly passed their censures; and voted this Address to his Majesty against Mr. Hutchinson and Mr. Oliver, upon account of a parcel of letters directed to somebody, they know not whom; and sent from somebody, they know not where. And Dr. Franklin now appears before your Lordships, wrapt up in impenetrable secresy, to support a charge against his Majesty's Governor and Lieutenant Governor; and expects that your Lordships should advise the punishing them, upon account of certain letters, which he *will* not produce, and which he *dares* not tell how he obtained.

But the Doctor says, *he transmitted them to his constituents.*

That Dr. Franklin sent these letters to such persons as he thought would in some way or other bring them into the Assembly, may be true. And accordingly, after an alarm of some dreadful discovery, these letters were produced by one single person, pretending to be under an injunction to observe the strictest secresy, and to suffer no copies to be taken of them. After allowing two or three days for fame to amplify, and for party malice to exaggerate; and after having thereby raised a general prejudice against the Governor; at length another Member tells the Assembly, that he had received from an unknown hand a *copy* of the letters; and wished to have that copy compared and authenticated with the originals. After this, when they had brought the Council into their measures, they then found their powers enlarged; and that they were at liberty to show them to any one, provided they did not suffer them to go out of their hands; and the King's Governor and Lieutenant Governor were permitted to look upon them only in this opprobrious manner, in order to render the indignity so much the more offensive.

This Dr. Franklin may call transmitting the letters to his constituents; and upon those who know nothing of the course of these proceedings, may easily impose the belief of it. But your Lordships will readily see, and every man who has been an agent very well knows, that this is not what is meant by transmitting to his constituents. My Lords, when an agent means to write to the

Assembly, he addresses his letter to the Speaker, to be communicated to the House. And the Doctor knows that there are many articles in the Journals of this tenor: " A letter from Dr. Franklin to the Speaker, was read."

But the course taken with these letters was just the reverse of this. The letter which came with them was anonymous; though the hand was well known: too well perhaps known to the selected few, who only were to be allowed the sight of it. Since therefore the Doctor has told us that he transmitted these letters to his constituents, we know now who they are. His constituents, by his own account, must be this particular junto; for to them, and them *only*, were the letters communicated. Dr. Franklin did *not* communicate them, as their agent, to the Assembly; for whatever may have been the whispers of this junto, the Assembly, as an Assembly, does not to this day know by whom the letters were sent. And so little do these innocent, well meaning farmers, which compose the bulk of the Assembly, know what they are about, that by the arts of these leaders, they have been brought to vote an Address to his Majesty to dismiss his Governor and Lieutenant Governor, founded upon certain papers, which they have not named; sent to them from somebody, they know not whom; and originally directed to somebody, they cannot tell where: for, my Lords, my accounts say, that it did not appear to the House that these letters had ever been in London.

I have pointed out to your Lordships the manner in which this conspiracy against the Governor was conducted, with all its circumstances, as the letters from Boston relate them. And from this account your Lordships will not wonder that I consider Dr. Franklin not so much in the light of an agent for the Assembly's purpose, as in that of a first mover and prime conductor of it for his own; not as the Assembly's agent for avenging this dreadful conspiracy of Mr. Hutchinson against his native country; but as the actor and secret spring, by which all the Assembly's motions were directed: the inventor and first planner of the whole contrivance. He it was that received and sent away Mr. Whately's letters. By what means he laid his hands on them he does not say; till he do, he leaves us at liberty to suppose the worst; I would wish to suggest the best. One case only must be excepted; Dr. Franklin will not add another injury, and say to the representative* of the Whately family, that *they* were any of them consenting to the perfidy. And yet, my Lords, nothing but that consent could put him honorably in possession of them, and much less give him a right to apply them to so unwarrantable a purpose.

My Lords, there is no end of this mischief. I have now in my hand an expostulatory letter from a Mr. Roome, not a native of America, but sent from London to Rhode Island, to collect in and sue for large outstanding debts there. This poor man, in a familiar letter to a friend in the same province, expresses a just indignation at the difficulties he met with in executing his trust, from the iniquitous tendency of their laws, and of the proceedings of their courts, to defraud their English creditors; and then gives him an invitation to come and spend some time with him at his country house, and catch perch and be of their fishing party. For this letter, the Assembly

---

* Mr. Whately intended, if he had been well enough, to have been at the Council.

brought him under examination, and committed him to prison, because he would not answer to his printed name at the end of one of the letters in this book.* Upon this occasion he writes a letter to one of his employers, with whom he had served his clerkship here in London, expostulating on the cruelty and injustice of the executors suffering their dead brother's papers to be applied to such a purpose. For he, my Lords, had no conception that any one else could have made this use of letters which did not belong to him. Mr. Roome had heard that the Boston letters had all been sent back again to London; and knew that their Speaker was directed to procure his original letter, in order to their proceeding against him still more severely. The merchant here came with this letter to a friend of Mr. Whately's, desiring that he would go with him to Mr. Whately, and join in entreating him not to send back the letter to their Speaker, which would oblige him, he writes, either to fly the Province, or else to suffer a long imprisonment. My Lords, Mr. Whately's friend had seen too much of the anguish of mind under which he had been suffering for the five months since this discovery. He knew that it would be giving him *another stab* to suffer a stranger abruptly to put this letter into his hands; he informed the merchant of the state of the affair, and prevented his going to him.

But what had this poor man done to Dr. Franklin, that *his* letter should be sent back too? Mr. Hutchinson and Mr. Oliver were public persons, and their letters, according to the Doctor's new code of morality, may be lawful prize. But Mr. Roome's is a name we had never heard

* The Book of Letters, printed at Boston, then in his hand.

of. Was *he* too a man in a public station? His friend, to whom he sent this invitation to come a fishing with him, was *he* a public person? Could Mr. Roome, when he was writing to New London, imagine that he was writing a letter to be shown to the King; and to alienate his affections from that loyal people? Did the sailing of the four regiments to Boston depend upon the intelligence of a man at Narragansett? The writer of this letter could not have a thought of its producing public measures. Surely then the returning of this letter might have been omitted; and this poor man at least might have been spared. But all men, be they in public stations or in private, be they great or small, all are prey that unfortunately fall into Dr. Franklin's hands : he wantonly and indiscriminately sends back the letters of all; unfeeling of the reflection which must arise in every other breast, that what is sport to him may be imprisonment and death to them.

But under all this weight of suspicion, in the full view of all the mischievous train of consequences which have followed from this treachery, (for such there must be somewhere, though Dr. Franklin does not choose to let us know where to fix it,) with a whole province set in a flame; with an honest, innocent man thrown into jail, and calling on Mr. Whately not to furnish the means of fixing him there; with a worthy family distressed, in the reflections cast on their own character, and in the sufferings brought upon their friends and correspondents; with the memory of one brother greatly injured, and the life of another greatly endangered; with all this weight of suspicion, and with all this train of mischiefs before his eyes, Dr. Franklin's apathy sets him quite at ease, and he would have us think that he has done nothing more than what any other Colony Agent would have done. He happened only to be the first Colony Agent who laid his hands on them, and he thought it his duty to transmit them to his constituents.

My Lords, I have the pleasure of knowing several very respectable gentlemen, who have been Colony Agents, and cannot but feel a little concern at seeing this strange imputation cast on that character. I have heard the sentiments of some of them. Upon being asked, whether, if they had laid their hands upon another gentleman's letters, they would have thought it their duty to make a like use of them: my Lords, they received the proposal with horror. One of them said, it was profaning the word *duty* to apply it to such a purpose; another, that if he had been their Agent, he would sooner have cut off his right hand than have done such a thing.

My Lords, Dr. Franklin's mind may have been so possessed with the idea of a Great American Republic, that he may easily slide into the language of the minister of a foreign independent state.* A foreign Ambassador when residing here, just before the breaking out of a war, or upon particular occasions, may bribe a villain to steal or betray any state papers; he is under the command of another state, and is not amenable to the laws of the country where he resides; and the secure exemption from punishment may induce a laxer morality.

But Dr. Franklin, whatever he may teach the people at Boston, while he is *here* at least is a subject; and if a subject injure a subject, he is answerable to the law.

* See also his Letter to Lord Dartmouth.

And the Court of Chancery will not much attend to his new self-created importance.

But, my Lords, the rank in which Dr. Franklin appears, is not even that of a Province Agent: he moves in a very inferior orbit. An agent for a province, your Lordships know, is a person chosen by the joint act of the Governor, Council, and Assembly; after which, a commission is issued by the Secretary, under the province seal, appointing him to that office. Such a real Colony Agent, being made by the joint concurrence of all the three branches of the Government, will think it his duty to consult the joint service of all the three; and to contribute all he can to the peace, harmony, and orderly government of the whole, as well as to the general welfare and prosperity of the province. This at least is what I learn from the copy books of two gentlemen, who at different periods were Agents for this very Colony. But Dr. Franklin's appointment seems to have been made in direct opposition to all these. Upon a message from the Council to the Assembly, desiring that they would join in the choice of an Agent for the Colony, they came to a resolution, that they would not join with the honorable Board in the choice of such an Agent; but resolved that they will choose an Agent of their own; and then, that Dr. Franklin should be that Agent. My Lords, the party by whom the Assembly is now directed, did not want a man who should think himself bound in duty to consult for the peace and harmony of the whole government; they had their own private separate views, and they wanted an Agent of their own, who should be a willing instrument and instructor in the accomplishing their own separate purposes. Dr. Franklin, therefore, your Lordships see, not only moves in a different orbit from that of other Colony Agents, but he gravitates also to a different centre. His great point appears to be to serve the interest of his party; and privately to supply the leaders of it with the necessary intelligence. Wheresoever and howsoever he can lay his hands on them, he thinks it his duty to furnish materials for dissensions; to set at variance the different branches of the Legislature; and to irritate and incense the minds of the King's subjects against the King's Governor.

But, says the Doctor, *the tendency of these letters was to incense the mother country against her colonies.*

There is a certain steadiness which is singularly remarkable in this case. These men are perpetually offering every kind of insult to the English nation. Setting the King's authority at defiance; treating the parliament as usurpers of an authority not belonging to them, and flatly denying the Supreme Jurisdiction of the British empire; and have been publishing their votes and resolutions for this purpose; and yet now pretend a great concern about these letters, as having a tendency to incense the parent state against the colony. Not content with bidding defiance to our authority, they now offer insult to our understanding; and at the very time while they are flying in the King's face, would have him turn out his Governor, because he has in the mildest terms intimated his opinion, that they do not pay the reverence they used to do, to the British authority.

My Lords, we are perpetually told of men's incensing the mother country against the colonies, of which I have never known a single instance. But we hear nothing of the vast variety of arts which have been made use of to incense the colonies against the mother country. And in all these arts no one I fear has been a more successful proficient, than the very man, who now stands forth as Mr. Hutchinson's accuser. My Lords, as he has been pleased in his own letter to avow this accusation, I shall now return the charge, and show to your Lordships who it is that is the true incendiary, and who is the great abettor of that faction at Boston, which, in form of a Committee of Correspondence, have been inflaming the whole province against his Majesty's government.

My Lords, the language of Dr. Franklin's peculiar correspondents is very well known. For years past they have been boasting of the countenance which he receives in England, and the encouragement which he sends over to them at Boston. One of their last boasted advices was: Go on, abstain from violence, but go on; for you have nothing to fear from the government here.

My Lords, from the excess of their zeal, these men are apt sometimes to let out a little too much. In the Boston Gazette of the 20th of September last is a letter, understood at Boston to have been written by Mr. Adams, one of Dr. Franklin's six constituents,[*] which ends with the following passage:—" The late Agent, Mr. De Bert, in one of his letters wrote, that Lord Hillsborough professed a great regard for the interest of America; and he thought the only thing that could be done to *serve* us, was *to keep the matter of right out of sight*. The *professed* design of that minister it seems was to serve us. But America has not yet thought it wise to agree to his Lord-

---

[*] This gentleman was the manager of the discovery of Mr. Hutchinson's letters in the Assembly; as Mr. Bowdoin, another of the six, was in the Council.

ship's political plan, to wink their liberties out of sight, for the sake of a temporary accommodation. Dr. Franklin, who is *perhaps* as penetrating a genius as his Lordship, extended his views a little farther. 'I hope,' says he, in a letter dated in 1771, ' the colony Assemblies will show by repeated resolves, *that they know their rights*, and *do not lose sight of them*. Our growing importance will ere long compel an acknowledgment of them, and establish and secure them *to our posterity.*' And he adds, 'I purpose to draw up a memorial *stating our rights and grievances*, and in the name and behalf of the province, *protesting particularly* against the late innovations. Whether speedy redress is or is not the consequence, I imagine it may be of good use *to keep alive our claims*, and *show* that we have not *given up* the contested points.' It seems to have been the judgment of this great man, that *a state of rights* should accompany a *complaint of grievances;* and that decent and manly protests against particular innovations, have the surest tendency to an effectual, if not a speedy removal of them." *

Your Lordships will be pleased to observe the time of Dr. Franklin's announcing his intention of drawing up for them such a memorial, was in 1771. At the proper season in the next year, there was produced a great work, under these very heads of a State of Rights, and a State of Grievances, and Protests against the new Innovations: but not from the press in London; that would not have answered the purpose. It was to be a memorial *in the name and behalf* of the province; and therefore was first to be sent thither, and receive the stamp of their authorities. A town meeting therefore was called, and a Com-

* This Gazette was misplaced during the speech.

mittee of Correspondence chosen, to draw up a state of their rights and grievances, and from the form of the resolution it is pretty manifest, that the leaders knew already what the work was to be. After an adjournment the Committee met, and produced this great twelve-penny book, under the very heads of a state of their rights, and containing a list of their grievances, with remonstrances sufficiently strong against what they call innovations. The work was received with the utmost applause, and instantly converted into votes and resolutions of the town of Boston. And doubtless it well deserved it. It is a set of ready drawn heads of a declaration for any one colony in America, or any one distant county in the kingdom, which shall choose to revolt from the British empire, and say that they will not be governed by the King and Parliament at Westminster. They therefore voted that this report of their Committee of Correspondence should be printed in a pamphlet, and that six hundred copies of them should be disposed of to the selectmen of the towns of the province, with an inflammatory letter, sounding *an alarm of a plan of despotism, with which the Administration* (and the Parliament) *intended to enslave them; and threatened them with certain and inevitable destruction;* and desiring that they would call town-meetings, and send their votes and resolutions upon this book. In sixty or seventy villages or townships such meetings had been held, and all express the highest approbation of this excellent performance. And well they might; for it told them a hundred rights, of which they never had heard before, and a hundred grievances which they never before had felt. Your Lordships see the votes and instructions of these several townships, in the Boston gazettes here before me. They are full of the most extravagant absurdities. Such as the enthusiastic rants of the wildest of my countrymen in the days of Charles II. cannot equal. It is impossible to read them to your Lordships. Those of Pembroke and of Marblehead are particularly curious: but I shall take those of the town of Petersham.

"*Resolved*, That the Parliament of Great Britain, usurping and exercising a legislative authority over, and extorting an unrighteous revenue from, these colonies, is against all divine and human laws. The late appointment of salaries to be paid to our Superior Court Judges, whose creation, pay, and commission, depend on mere will and pleasure, complete a system of bondage equal to any ever before fabricated by the combined efforts of the ingenuity, malice, fraud, and wickedness of man.

" Therefore, *Resolved*, That it is the first and highest social duty of this people, to consider of, and seek ways and means for a speedy redress of these mighty grievances and intolerable wrongs; and that for the obtainment of this end, this people are warranted, by the laws of God and nature, in the use of every rightful art, and energy of *policy, stratagem, and force*.

" Therefore, it is our earnest desire, and we here direct you, to use your utmost influence (as one of the legislative body) to convince the nation of Great Britain that the measures that they have meted out to us, will have a direct tendency to destroy both them and us; and petition the King and Parliament of Great Britain, in the most pathetic and striking manner, to relieve us from our aggravated grievances; but if all this should fail, we recommend it to your consideration, and direct you to move it to the consideration of the honorable Court, whether it would not be best to *call in the aid of some Protestant power or powers,* requesting that they would use their kind and Christian influence with our mother country, that so we may be relieved, and that brotherly love and harmony may again take place."

These are the lessons taught in Dr. Franklin's school of Politics. My Lords, I do not say that Dr. Franklin is the original author of this book. But your Lordships will give me leave to observe, in the first place, that it is not very likely that any of the Doctor's scholars at Boston, should attempt to draw up such a state of rights and grievances, when the *great man,* their master, had given them notice that he should himself set about such a work; and, in the next place, that if the Doctor should not choose now to filiate the child, yet the time has been when he was not ashamed of it; for, after it had had its operation in America, the Doctor reprinted it here, with a preface of his own, and presented it to his friends.

My Lords, I have said that sixty or seventy of the townships had already voted their approbation of the book. The evil was catching from town to town (and if the greater part could have been engaged, they would have forced the rest) when the Governor thought it his duty to interpose. He therefore called upon the Assembly to disown these undutiful proceedings. Had he only mentioned the disloyalty and evil tendency of them, they would probably have passed a few resolutions, and have suffered the evil to go on. He was well aware, that the Assembly could easily vote themselves as many privileges as they pleased, but that it was not so easy to prove their right to them. He, therefore, disarmed them of their strength in voting, and put them under the necessity of proving; and there he knew they would fail. By opening the session with that very masterly speech in defence of the British-American constitution, he, for a time, stunned the faction, and gave a check to the progress of their town-meetings. And though the same men were in the Assembly created a Committee of Correspondence, to write to the Assemblies of the other provinces, yet the spirit of the design languished, and but little more was then done in it.

This, my Lords, is the great and principal ground of their quarrel with Mr. Hutchinson. They want a Governor who shall know *less* than themselves, whereas he makes them feel that he knows *more*. He stopped the train which Dr. Franklin's constituents had laid, to blow up the province into a flame, which from thence was to have been spread over the other provinces. This was the real provocation: and for this they have been seeking for some ground of accusation against him.

After sifting his whole conduct for the four years in which he has been Governor, they are not able to point out a single action to find fault with. Their only recourse is to their own surmises of what were the sentiments of his heart five or six years ago. *He was,* they say, *among the instruments in introducing a fleet and army into the province.* Have they attempted any proof of this? No. But they fancy it from some letters of his, which do not say a single word of that sort. Is it possible to conceive of a more groundless accusation, or not to see their intent in it?

My Lords, they mean nothing more by this Address, than to fix a stigma on the Governor by the accusation.

Their charge, founded upon a pretence of knowing six years ago what were Mr. Hutchinson's thoughts, is not really designed for his Majesty in Council. They know that your Lordships will not take an accusation for a proof; nor condemn without evidence. They never desired to be brought to a hearing; and therefore the first instant when your Lordships call for their proofs, they fly off, and say they do not mean this as a charge, or a trial before your Lordships; and they say truly : they meant to bring it before the multitude, and to address the popular prejudices. The mob, they know, need only hear their Governors accused, and *they* will be sure to condemn. My Lords, they boast at Boston, that they have found this method succeed against their last Governor, and they hope to make it do against this; and by a second precedent to establish their power, and make all future Governors bow to their authority. They wish to erect themselves into a tyranny greater than the Roman : to be able, sitting in their own secret cabal, to dictate for the Assembly, and send away their *verbosa et grandis epistola*, and get even a *virtuous* Governor dragged from his seat, and made the sport of a Boston mob.

Having turned out all other Governors, they may at length hope to get one of their own. The letters from Boston, for two years past, have intimated that Dr. Franklin was aiming at Mr. Hutchinson's government. It was not easy before this to give credit to such surmises : but nothing surely but a too eager attention to an ambition of this sort, could have betrayed a wise man into such a conduct as we have now seen. Whether these surmises are true or not, your Lordships are much the best judges. If they should be true, I hope that

Mr. Hutchinson will not meet with the less countenance from your Lordships, for his *rival's* being his accuser. Nor will your Lordships, I trust, from what you have heard, advise the having Mr. Hutchinson displaced, in order to make room for Dr. Franklin as a successor.

With regard to his *constituents*, the factious leaders at Boston, who make this complaint against their Governor; if the *relating* of their evil doings be criminal, and tending to alienate his Majesty's affections, must not the *doing* of them be much more so? Yet now they ask that his Majesty will gratify and reward *them* for doing these things; and that he will punish their Governor for relating them, because they are so very bad that it cannot but offend his Majesty to hear of them.

My Lords, if the account given in these letters, of their proceedings five years ago, tended to alienate his Majesty's affections, has their conduct ever since been in any respect more conciliating? Was it to confute or prevent the pernicious effect of these letters, that the good men of Boston have lately held their meetings, appointed their Committees, and with their usual moderation destroyed the cargo of three British ships? If an English Consul, in any part of France or Spain, or rather Algiers or Tripoli, (for European Powers respect the law of nations,) had not called this an outrage on his country, he would have deserved punishment. But if a Governor at Boston should presume to whisper to a friend, that he thinks it somewhat more than a moderate exertion of English liberty, to destroy the ships of England, to attack her officers, to plunder their goods, to pull down their houses, or even to burn the King's ships of war, he ought to be removed; because such a conduct in him *has a natural and efficacious tendency to interrupt the harmony between Great Britain and the colony*, which these good subjects are striving by such means to establish.

On the part of Mr. Hutchinson and Mr. Oliver, I am instructed to assure your Lordships, that they feel no spark of resentment, even at the individuals who have done them this injustice. Their private letters breathe nothing but moderation. They are convinced that the *people*, though misled, are innocent. If the conduct of a few should provoke a just indignation, *they* would be the most forward, and, I trust, the most efficacious solicitors to avert its effects, and to excuse the men. They love the soil, the constitution, the people of New England; they look with reverence to this country, and with affection to that. For the sake of the people they wish some faults corrected, anarchy abolished, and government re-established. But these salutary ends they wish to promote by the gentlest means; and the abridging of no liberties, which a people can possibly use to its own advantage. A restraint from self-destruction is the only restraint they desire to be imposed upon New England.

My Lords, I have said that the letter which accompanied these in question, was anonymous, and that it was directed to be shown to six persons only.

I am prepared to enter into the proof of this. I call upon Dr. Franklin, for my witness. And I am ready to examine him.

N. B.—Dr. Franklin being present, remained silent, but declared by his counsel that he did not choose to be examined.

The following letter having been mentioned in Mr. Wedderburn's Speech, it is printed for the reader's satisfaction, and to complete the collection.

Copy of a Letter returned with those signed Tho. Hutchinson, Andrew Oliver, &c.

FROM ENGLAND.

Narraganset, Dec. 22, 1767.

SIR :—I am now withdrawn to my little country villa, where, though I am more retired from the busy world, yet I am still enveloped with uneasy reflections for a turbulent, degenerate, ungrateful continent, and the opposition I have met with in my indefatigable endeavors to secure our property in this colony, but hitherto without success. The times are so corrupted, and the conflict of parties so predominant, that faction is blind, or shuts her eyes to the most evident truths that cross her designs, and believes in any absurdities that assists to accomplish her purposes under the prostitution and prostration of an infatuated government. Judge then, my dear sir, in what a critical situation the fortunes of *we* poor Europeans must be among them.

We have not been able to recover our property for years past, how great soever our exigencies may have been, unless we soothed them into a compliance. We are unwilling to enter into a litis-contestation with them, because the perversion of their iniquitous courts of justice are so great, that experience has convinced us we had better lose half, to obtain the other quietly, than pursue compulsory measures. We are also afraid to apply to a British parliament for relief, as none can be effectually

administered without a change of government, and a
better administration of justice introduced; and was it
known here that we made such application home, not only
our fortunes would be in greater jeopardy, but our lives
endangered by it before any salutary regulations could
take place. We are sensible of the goodness of the King
and Parliament, but how far, or in what space of time
our grievance, as a few individuals, might weigh against
the influence of a charter government, we are at a loss to
determine.

In 1761, I arrived in America, which circumstance you
probably remember well. With great industry, caution
and circumspection, I have not only reduced our demands,
and regulated our connections in some measure, but kept
my head out of a *halter* which you had the honor to grace.
(Pray, Doctor, how did it feel? The subject is stale,
but I must be a little funny with you on the occasion.)
Much still remains to be done, and after all my best endeavors, my constituents, from a moderate calculation,
cannot lose less than £50,000 sterling, by the baneful
constitution of this colony, and corruption of their courts
of judicature. *It is really a very affecting and melancholy
consideration.*

Under a deep sense of the infirmities of their constitution; the innovations which they have gradually inter-
woven among themselves: and stimulated by every act
of forbearance, lenity, and patience, we have indulged
our correspondents until deluges of bankruptcies have
ensued, insolvent acts liberated them from our just demands, and finally, had our indisputable accounts refused
admission for our proportion of the small remains, until
colony creditors were first paid, and the whole absorbed.

We have had vessels made over to us for the satisfaction of debts, and after bills of sales were executed, carried off in open violence and force by Capt. Snip-snap of Mr. Nobody's appointment, and when we sued him for damages, recovered a louse. We have in our turn been sued in our absence, and condemned *ex parte* in large sums for imaginary damages, for which we can neither obtain a trial, nor redress. They refuse us an appeal to the king in council; the money must be paid when their executions become returnable; and were we to carry it home by way of complaint, it would cost us two or three hundred pounds sterling to prosecute, and after all, when his Majesty's decrees come over in our favor, and refunding the money can no longer be evaded, I expect their effects will be secreted, their bodies released by the insolvent act, and our money, both principal, interest, and expenses, irrecoverably gone. Is not our case grievous? We have in actions, founded upon notes of hand, been cast in their courts of judicature. We have appealed to his Majesty in council for redress, got their verdicts reversed, and obtained the king's decrees for our money, but *that is all;* for although I have had them by me above twelve months, and employed two eminent lawyers to enforce them into execution, conformable to the colony law, yet we have not been able to recover a single shilling, though we have danced after their courts and assemblies above *thirty days*, *in vain* to accomplish that purpose only. Consider, my dear Sir, what expense, vexation, and loss of time this must be to us, and whether we have not just cause of complaint.

We have also in vain waited with great impatience for years past, in hopes his Majesty would have nominated his judges, and other executive officers in every colony in America, which would in a great measure have removed the cause of our complaint. Nothing can be more necessary than a speedy regulation in this, and constituting it a regal government; and nothing is of such important use to a nation, as that men who excel in *wisdom* and *virtue* should be encouraged to undertake the business of government. But the iniquitous course of their courts of justice in this colony deters such men from serving the public, or if they do so, unless patronized at home, their wisdom and virtue are turned against them with such malignity, that it is more safe to be *infamous* than renowned. The principal exception I have met with here, is James Helmes, Esq., who was chosen chief justice by the General Assembly at last election. He accepted his appointment, distinguishes himself by capacity and application, and seems neither afraid nor ashamed to administer impartial justice to *all*, even to the native and residing creditors of the mother country. I have known him grant them temporary relief by writs of error, &c., when both he and they were overruled by the partiality of the court; and in vain, though with great candor and force, plead with the rest of the bench, that for the honor of the colony, and their own reputation, they ought never to pay less regard to the decrees of his Majesty in council, because the property was determined in Great Britain, than to their own. I have also heard him with *resolution and firmness*, when he discovered the court to be *immoderately partial*, order his name to be enrolled, as dissenting from the verdict. For such honesty and candor, I am persuaded he will be deposed at next election, unless they should be still in hopes of making a convert of him.

I wish it was in my power to prevent every American from suffering for the cause of integrity and their mother country; *he*, in an especial manner, should not only be *protected* and *supported*, but appear among the first promotions. Is there no gentleman of public spirit at home, that would be pleased to be an instrument of elevating a man of his principles and probity? Or is it become fashionable for vice to be countenanced with impunity, and every trace of virtue passed over unnoticed? God forbid!

The colonies have originally been wrong founded. They ought all to have been regal governments, and every executive officer appointed by the king. Until that is effected, and they are properly regulated, they will never be beneficial to themselves, nor good subjects to Great Britain. You see with what contempt they already treat the acts of parliament for regulating their trade, and enter into the most public, illegal, and affronting combinations to obtain a repeal, by again imposing upon the British merchants and manufacturers, and all under the cloak of *retrenching their expenses* by avoiding every *unnecessary superfluity*. Were that really the case, I am sure I would, and also every other British subject, esteem them for it; but the fact is, they obtained a repeal of the stamp act by mercantile influence, and they are now endeavoring by the same artifice and finesse to repeal the acts of trade, and obtain a total exemption from all taxation. Were it otherways, and they sincerely disposed to stop the importation of every unnecessary superfluity, without affronting the British legislation by their public, general, and illegal combinations, they might accomplish their purposes with much more *decency*, and suppress it more effectually by the acts of their own legislation, imposing such duties upon their importation here,* as might either occasion a total prohibition, or confine the consumption of them to particular individuals that can afford to buy, by which measures they would also raise a considerable colony *Revenue*, and ease the poor inhabitants in the tax they now pay. But the temper of the country is exceedingly *factious*, and prone to sedition; they are growing more *imperious, haughty*, nay *insolent* every day, and in a short space, unless wholesome regulations take place, the spirit they have enkindled, and the conceptions of government they have imbibed, will be more grievous to the mother country than ever the ostracism was to the Athenians.

A bridle at present may accomplish more than a rod hereafter; for the malignant poison of the times, like a general pestilence, spreads beyond conception; and if the British parliament are too late in their regulations, neglect measures seven years, which are essentially necessary now, should they then be able to stifle their commotions, it will only be a temporary extinction, consequently, every hour's indulgence will answer no other purpose than to enable them in a more effectual manner to sow seeds of dissension to be rekindled whenever they are in a capacity to oppose the mother country and render themselves independent of her.

Have they not already in the most public manner shown their opposition to the measures of parliament in the affair of the late stamp act? Do not they now with equal violence and audacity, in both public papers and conversa-

* I mean foreign growth or fabrications; but if on British, it would be more pardonable than their present system.

tion, declare the parliamentary regulations in their acts of trade to be illegal and a mere nullity? What further proofs do we wait for, of either their good or bad disposition? Did you ever hear of any colonies, *in their infant state*, teach the science of tyranny, *reduced into rules*,* over every subject that discountenanced their measures in opposition to the mother country, *in a more imperious manner than they have done these four years past?*

Have they not made use of every stroke of policy (in their way) to avail themselves of the dark purposes of their independence, and suffered no restraint of conscience, or fear, not even the guilt of threatening *to excite a civil war*, and *revolt*, if not indulged with an unlimited trade, without restraint; and British protection, without expence? for that is the engine of it. Is this their true or mistaken portrait? SAY. If it is their true one, ought not such pernicious maxims of policy—such wicked discipline—such ingratitude—such dissimulation—such perfidy—such violent, ruthless and sanguinary councils, where a Cleon bears rule, and an Aristides cannot be endured, to be crushed in embryo? If not, the alternative cannot avoid producing such a government, as will ere long throw the whole kingdom into the utmost confusion, endanger the life, liberty, and property of every good subject, and again expose them to the merciless assassination of a rabble.

I am sensible that in all political disputes, especially in America, a man may see some things to blame on both sides, and so much to fear, which every faction should conquer, as to be justified in not intermeddling with either; but in matters of such vast importance as the

---

* The Committee to the Sons of Liberty, &c.

present, wherein we have suffered so much—still deeply interested, and by which the peace and tranquillity of the nation is at stake; it is difficult to conceal one's emotions from a friend, and remain a tranquil spectator on a theatre of such chicanery and collusion as will inevitably (if not checked, and may sooner happen than is imagined by many) chill the blood of many a true Briton.

It may be true policy, in some cases, to tame the fiercest spirit of popular liberty, not by blows, or by chains, but by soothing her into a willing obedience, and making her kiss the very hand that restrains her; but such policy would be a very unsuitable potion to cure the malady of the present times. They are too much corrupted, and already so intoxicated with their own importance as to make a wrong use of lenient measures. They construe them into their own natural rights, and a timidity in the mother country. They consider themselves a little bigger than the *frog* in the *fable*, and that Great Britain can never long grapple with their huge territory of 1500 miles frontier, already populous, and increasing with such celerity, as to double their numbers once in *twenty-five years*. This is not perfectly consonant with my idea of the matter, though such calculation has been made; and admitting it to be erroneous, yet as they believe it, it has the same evil effect, and possesses the imaginations of the people with such a degree of insanity and enthusiasm, as there is hardly anything more common than to hear them boast of particular colonies that can raise on a short notice *an hundred thousand fighting men to oppose the force of Great Britain;* certain it is, that they increase in numbers by emigration, &c., very fast, and are become such a body of people, with such extensive territory as require every bud of their genius and disposition to be narrowly watched and pruned with great judgment, otherwise they may become, not only troublesome to Great Britain, but enemies to themselves. Now is the critical season. They are still like some raw, giddy youth just emerging into the world, in a corrupt, degenerate age. A parent, or a guardian, is therefore still necessary; and if well managed, they will soon arrive at such maturity as to become obedient, dutiful children; but if neglected long, the rod of chastisement will be so much longer necessary as to become too burthensome, and must be dropped with the colonies. They almost consider themselves as a separate people from Great Britain already.

Last month, while I was attending the General Assembly, the Governor sent a written message to the lower house, importing his intention of a resignation at the next election, assigning for reasons, the fumes in the colony and party spirit were so high, and that bribery and corruption were so predominant, that neither *life, liberty*, nor *property*, were safe, &c., &c., &c. Now, Sir, whether the Governor's intentions, as exhibited in this open, public declaration was real or *feigned*, to answer political purposes, it still evinces their decrepid state, the prostitution of government, and melancholy situation of every good subject: For it cannot be supposed, by any candid inquisitor, that a declaration of that nature and form would, if not true, have been delivered by a Governor to a whole legislative body in order to emancipate himself. If this truth is granted, and this allowed to be their unhappy situation, how much is it the duty of every good man, and what language is sufficient to paint, in an effectual manner, this internal imbecility of an English colony (in many other respects favorably situated for trade and commerce, one of the safest, largest, and most commodious harbors in all America, or perhaps in all Europe, accessible at all seasons, situated in a fine climate, and abounding with fertile soil) to the maternal bowels of compassion in order that she may seasonably, if she thinks it necessary to interpose, regulate, and wipe away their pernicious Charter, rendered obnoxious by the abuse of it!

I am afraid I have tired your patience with a subject that must give pain to every impartial friend to Great Britain and her colonies. When I took up my pen, I only intended to have communicated the outlines of such of my perplexities (without dipping so far into political matter) as I thought would atone for, or excuse my long silence, and excite your compassion and advice.

Our friend Robinson is gone to Boston to join the commissioners. My compliments to Colonel Stuart. May I ask the favor of you both to come and eat a Christmas dinner with me at Batchelor's hall, and celebrate the festivity of the season with me in Narraganset woods. A covy of partridges, or bevy of quails, will be entertainment for the Colonel and me, while the pike and perch ponds amuse you. Should business or pre-engagement prevent me that pleasure, permit me to ask the favor of your earliest intelligence of the proceedings of parliament, and of your opinion whether our case is not so grievous as to excite their compassion and interposition, were it known? This narration, together with your own knowledge of many of the facts, and the disposition of the colonies in general, will refresh your memory and enable you to form a judgment. Relief from home seems so tedious, especially to us who have suffered so much, like to suffer more, and unacquainted with their reasons of delay, that I am quite impatient.

Above twelve months ago, I received from three gentlemen in London (in trust for several others) exemplified accounts for a balance of above twenty-six thousand pounds sterling, mostly due from this colony, not £50 of which shall I ever be able to recover without compulsive measures, and what is still worse, my lawyer advises me from all thoughts of prosecution unless a change of government ensues. I am therefore obliged to send them his opinion (in justification of my own conduct) in lieu of money ten years due. Poor satisfaction! Our consolation must be in a British parliament. Every other avenue is rendered impregnable by their subtlety and degeneracy, and we can no longer depend upon a people who are so unthankful for our indulgences, and the lenity of their mother country. I wish you the compliments of the approaching season, and a succession of many happy new years.

I am, Sir, with much regard,
Your most humble Servant,
G. ROME.

At the Court at ST. JAMES'S, *the 7th day of February,* 1774.

PRESENT.

The KING's most Excellent Majesty,

Lord Chancellor,
Lord President,
Duke of Queensberry,
Duke of Ancaster,
Lord Chamberlain,
Earl of Suffolk,
Earl of Denbigh,
Earl of Sandwich,
Earl of Rochford,
Earl of Dartmouth,
Earl of Bristol,
Earl of Pomfret,

Viscount Falmouth,
Viscount Barrington,
Lord Le Despenser,
Lord Cathcart,
Lord Hyde,
James Stuart Mackenzie, Esq.,
Hans Stanley, Esq.,
George Onslow, Esq.,
Sir Jeffery Amherst,
Charles Jenkinson, Esq.,
Sir John Goodricke.

Whereas there was this day read at the Board, a Report from the Right Honorable the Lords of the Committee of Council for Plantation Affairs, dated the 29th of last month, in the words following, viz:

"At the Council Chamber, Whitehall, the 29th of January, 1774.

"By the Right Honorable the Lords of the Committee of Council for Plantation Affairs.

PRESENT.

Archbishop of Canterbury,
Lord President,
Duke of Queensberry,
Earl of Suffolk,
Earl of Denbigh,
Earl of Sandwich,
Lord Geo. Sackville Jermain,

Earl of Rochford,
Earl of Marchmont,
Earl of Dartmouth,
Earl of Buckinghamshire,
Earl of Hardwicke,
Earl of Hillsborough,
Hans Stanley, Esq.,

Viscount Townshend,	Richard Rigby, Esq.,
Viscount Falmouth,	Sir Eardly Wilmot,
Lord North,	Thomas Townsend, jr., Esq.,
Bishop of London,	George Onslow, Esq.,
Lord Le Despencer,	George Rice, Esq.,
Lord Cathcart,	Lord Chief Justice De Grey,
Lord Hyde,	Sir Lawrence Dundass,
James Stuart Mackenzie, Esq.,	Sir Jeffery Amherst,
General Conway,	Sir Thomas Parker,
Wellbore Ellis, Esq.,	Charles Jenkinson, Esq.
Sir Gilbert Elliott,	

"Your Majesty having been pleased by your Order in Council of the 10th of last month, to refer unto this Committee an Address of the House of Representatives of the Province of Massachusetts Bay, complaining of the conduct of Thomas Hutchinson, Esq., Governor, and Andrew Oliver, Esq., Lieutenant Governor of that Province; and humbly praying that your Majesty would be pleased to remove the said Thomas Hutchinson, Esq., and Andrew Oliver, Esq., from their posts in that government: the Lords of the Committee did, in obedience to your Majesty's said order of reference, proceed on the 11th of this instant, to take the petition of the said House of Representatives into consideration, and were attended by Benjamin Franklin, Esquire, styling himself agent for the said House of Representatives, (and from whom the said petition had been transmitted to the Right Honorable the Earl of Dartmouth, one of your Majesty's principal Secretaries of State,) and likewise by Israel Mauduit, Esquire, from whom application had been made to this Committee, humbly praying on behalf of your Majesty's said Governor and Lieutenant Governor, that he might be heard by Council in relation to the Address of the House of Representatives of the said province; and the said Benjamin

Franklin, Esq., having thereupon prayed, that he might in that case be heard also by his Council at a future day: the Lords of the Committee did, in compliance with the petition of the said Israel Mauduit, Esq., and at the instance of the said Benjamin Franklin, Esq., think proper to appoint a future day to resume the consideration of the said petition of the House of Representatives of Massachusetts Bay, and to allow Council to be heard on both sides thereupon. And their Lordships having been this day attended by Council on both sides accordingly, and heard all that they had to offer, and having maturely weighed and considered the whole of the evidence adduced by the said Benjamin Franklin, Esq., upon which the said House of Representatives did come to the several resolves, which are the foundation of their said petition to your Majesty : the Lords of the Committee take leave to represent to your Majesty, that the said House of Representatives have by their said petition taken upon themselves to bring a general charge against your Majesty's said Governor and Lieutenant Governor, and to complain of their conduct, 'As having a natural and efficacious tendency to interrupt and alienate the affections of your Majesty from that your loyal Province—to destroy that harmony and good-will between Great Britain and that Colony, which every honest subject would strive to establish—to excite the resentment of the British administration against that province—to defeat the endeavors of their agents and friends to serve them by a fair representation of their state of facts—to prevent their humble and repeated petitions from reaching the ear of your Majesty, or having their desired effect ; and finally charging your Majesty's said Governor and Lieutenant Governor with having been among the chief instruments of introducing a fleet and an army into that province, to establish and perpetuate their plans; whereby your Majesty's said Governor and Lieutenant Governor have been not only greatly instrumental of disturbing the peace and harmony of the government, and causing unnatural and hateful discords and animosities between the several parts of your Majesty's extensive dominions; but are justly chargeable with all that corruption of morals, and all that confusion, misery, and bloodshed, which have been the natural effects of posting an army in a populous town.' But the Lords of the Committee cannot but express their astonishment, that a charge of so serious and extensive a nature against the persons whom the said House of Representatives acknowledge by their said petition to have heretofore had the confidence and esteem of the people, and to have been advanced by your Majesty from the purest motives of rendering your subjects happy, to the highest places of trust and authority in that province, should have no other evidence to support it but inflammatory and precipitate resolutions, founded only on certain letters, written respectively by them (and all but one before they were appointed to the posts they now hold) in the years 1767, 1768, and 1769, to a gentleman then in no office under the government, in the course of familiar correspondence, and in the confidence of private friendship, and which it was said (and it was not denied by Mr. Franklin) were surreptitiously obtained after his death, and sent over to America, and laid before the Assembly of the Massachusetts Bay; and which letters appear to us to contain nothing reprehensible or unworthy of the situation they were in; and we presume, that it was from this impropriety, that the Council did disclaim on behalf of the Assembly any intention of bringing a criminal charge against the Governor and Lieutenant Governor; but said that the petition was founded solely on the ground of the Governor and Lieutenant Governor being, as they alleged, now become obnoxious to the people of the province; and that it was in this light only that the said petition was presented to your Majesty. And there being no other evidence now produced, than the said resolutions and letters, together with resolutions of a similar import by the Council of the said province, founded, as it was said, on the same letters—

"The Lords of the Committee do agree humbly to report, as their opinion to your Majesty, that the said petition is founded upon resolutions, formed upon false and erroneous allegations, and that the same is groundless, vexatious, and scandalous, and calculated only for the seditious purposes of keeping up a spirit of clamor and discontent in the said province. And the Lords of the Committee do further humbly report to your Majesty, that nothing has been laid before them, which does or can, in their opinion, in any manner or in any degree, impeach the honor, integrity, or conduct of the said Governor or Lieutenant Governor; and their Lordships are humbly of opinion, that the said petition ought to be dismissed."

His Majesty taking the said report into consideration, was pleased, with the advice of his Privy Council, to approve thereof; and to order, that the said petition of the

House of Representatives of the province of the Massachusetts Bay, be, and it is hereby dismissed this Board, as groundless, vexatious, and scandalous, and calculated only for the seditious purpose of keeping up a spirit of clamor and discontent in the said province.

G. CHETWYND.

THE SPEECH

OF THE RIGHT HONORABLE

THE EARL OF CHATHAM, &C.

My Lords :—After more than six weeks' possession of the papers now before you, on a subject so momentous, at a time when the state of this nation hangs on every hour; the Ministry have at length condescended to submit to the consideration of the House intelligence from America, with which your Lordships and the public have been long and fully acquainted.

The measures of last year, my Lords, which have produced the present alarming state of America, were founded upon misrepresentation—they were violent, precipitate, and vindictive. The nation was told that it was only a faction in Boston, which opposed all lawful government; that an unwarrantable injury had been done to private property, for which the justice of Parliament was called upon, to order reparation; that the least appearance of firmness would awe the Americans into submission, and upon only passing the Rubicon, we should be, *sine clade victor.*

That the people might choose their Representatives under the impression of those misrepresentations, the Parliament was precipitately dissolved. Thus the nation was to be rendered instrumental in executing the vengeance of Administration on that injured, unhappy, traduced people.

But now, my Lords, we find, that instead of suppressing the opposition of the faction at Boston, these measures have spread it over the whole continent. They have united that whole people by the most indissoluble of all bands—intolerable wrongs. The just retribution is an indiscriminate, unmerciful proscription of the innocent with the guilty, unheard and untried. The bloodless victory is an impotent general with his dishonored army, trusting solely to the pick-axe and the spade, for security against the just indignation of an injured and insulted people.

My Lords, I am happy that a relaxation of my infirmities permits me to seize this earliest opportunity of offering my poor advice to save this unhappy country, at this moment tottering to its ruin. But, as I have not the honor of access to his Majesty, I will endeavor to transmit to him through the constitutional channel of this House, *my* ideas on American business, to rescue him from the misadvice of his present Ministers. I congratulate your Lordships, that *that* business is at last entered upon, by the noble Lord's (Lord Dartmouth) laying the papers before you. As I suppose your Lordships are too well apprised of their contents, I hope I am not premature in submitting to you my present motion, [reads the motion]; I wish my Lords not to lose a day in this urging present crisis: an hour now lost in allaying the ferment in America, may produce years of calamity; but for my own part, I will not desert for a moment the conduct of this mighty business from the first to the last, unless nailed to my bed by the extremity of sickness; I will give it unremitting attention: I will knock at the door of this sleeping, or confounded Ministry, and will rouse them to a sense of their important danger. When I state the importance of the colonies to this country, and the magnitude of danger hanging over this country from the present plan of misadministration practiced against them, I desire not to be understood to argue for a reciprocity of *indulgence* between England and America: I contend not for indulgence, but justice, to America; and I shall ever contend that the Americans justly owe obedience to us, in a limited degree; they owe obedience to our ordinances of trade and navigation; but let the line be skilfully drawn between the objects of those ordinances, and their private, internal property: let the sacredness of their property remain inviolate; let it be taxable only by their own consent, given in their provincial assemblies, else it will cease to be property. As to the metaphysical refinements attempting to show that the Americans are equally free from obedience to commercial restraints, as from taxation for revenue, as being unrepresented here, I pronounce them futile, frivolous, and groundless. Property is, in its nature, single as an atom. It is indivisible, can belong to one only, and cannot be touched but by his consent. The law that attempts to alter this disposal of it annihilates it.

When I urge this measure of recalling the troops from Boston, I urge it on this pressing principle—that it is necessarily preparatory to the restoration of your peace, and the re-establishment of your prosperity. It will then appear that you are disposed to treat amicably and equitably, and to consider, revise, and repeal, if it should be found necessary, as I affirm it will, those violent acts and declarations which have disseminated confusion throughout your empire. Resistance to your acts was as necessary as it was just; and your vain declarations of the omnipotence of Parliament, and your imperious doctrines of the necessity of submission, will be found equally impotent to convince or enslave your fellow-subjects in America, who feel that tyranny, whether ambitioned by an individual part of the Legislature, or by the bodies which compose it, is equally intolerable to British principles.

As to the means of enforcing this thraldom, they are found to be as ridiculous and weak in practice, as they were unjust in principle. Indeed I cannot but feel with the most anxious sensibility, for the situation of General Gage and the troops under his command; thinking him, as I do, a man of humanity and understanding, and entertaining, as I ever shall, the highest respect, the warmest love, for the British troops. Their situation is truly unworthy, pent up, pining in inglorious inactivity. They are an army of impotence. You may call them an army of safety and of guard; but they are in truth an army of impotence and contempt—and to render the folly equal to the disgrace, they are an army of irritation. I do not mean to censure the inactivity of the troops. It is a prudent and a necessary inaction. But it is a miserable condition, where disgrace is prudence; and where it is necessary to be contemptible. This tameness, however disgraceful, ought not to be blamed, as I am surprised to hear is done by these Ministers. The first drop of blood, shed in a civil and unnatural war, would be an *immedicabile vulnus*. It would entail hatred and contention between the two people, from generation to generation. Woe be to him who sheds the first—the unexpiable—drop of blood in an impious war, with a people contending in the great cause of public liberty. I will tell you plainly, my Lords, no son of mine, nor any one over whom I have influence, shall ever draw his sword upon his fellow subjects.

I therefore urge and conjure your Lordships immediately to adopt this conciliatory measure. I will pledge myself for its immediately producing conciliatory effects, from its being well timed. But if you delay till your vain hope of triumphantly dictating the terms shall be accomplished, you delay forever. And even admitting that this hope, which in truth is desperate, should be accomplished, what will you gain by a victorious imposition of amity? You will be untrusted and unthanked. Adopt then the grace, while you have the opportunity of reconcilement, or at least prepare the way; allay the ferment prevailing in America, by removing the obnoxious hostile cause. Obnoxious and unserviceable; for their merit can be only inaction. "Non dimicare est vincere." Their victory can never be by exertions. Their force would be most disproportionately exerted, against a brave, generous, and united people; with arms in their hands and courage in their hearts; three millions of people, the genuine descendants of a valiant and pious ancestry, driven to these deserts by the narrow maxims of a superstitious tyranny. And is the spirit of tyrannous persecution never to be appeased? Are the brave sons of those brave forefathers to inherit their sufferings, as they have inherited their virtues? Are they to sustain the inflictions of the most oppressive and unexampled severity, beyond the accounts of history or the description of poetry? " Rhadamanthus habet durissima regna, Castigatque *auditque.*" So says the wisest statesman and politician. But the Bostonians have been condemned *unheard.* The indiscriminating hand of vengeance has lumped together innocent and guilty : with all the formalities of hostility, has blocked up the town, and reduced to beggary and famine 30,000 inhabitants. But his Majesty is advised that the union of America cannot last. Ministers have more eyes than I, and should have more ears, but from all the information I have been able to procure, I can pronounce it a union solid, permanent, and effectual. Ministers may satisfy themselves and delude the public with the reports of what they call commercial bodies in America. They are not commercial. They are your packers and factors; they live upon nothing, for I call commission nothing; I mean the ministerial *authority* for their American intelligence — the runners of government, who are paid for their intelligence. But these are not the men, nor this the influence to be considered in America, when we estimate the firmness of their union. Even to extend the question, and to take in the really mercantile circle, will be totally inadequate to the consideration. Trade indeed increases the wealth and glory of a country; but its real strength and stamina are to be looked for among the cultivators of the land. In their simplicity of life is found the simplicity of virtue, the integrity and courage of freedom. Those true genuine sons of the earth are invincible; and they surround and hem in the mercantile bodies; even if those bodies, which supposition I totally disclaim, could be supposed disaffected to the cause of liberty. Of this general spirit existing in the American *nation*, for so I wish to distinguish the real and genuine Americans from the pseudo-traders I have described: of this spirit of independence animating the *nation* of America, I have the most authentic information. It is not new among them; it is, and ever has been, their established principle, their confirmed persuasion; it is their nature and their doctrine. I remember some years ago when the repeal of the Stamp Act was in agitation, conversing in a friendly confidence with a person of undoubted respect and authenticity on this subject; and he assured me with a certainty which his judgment and opportunity gave him, that these were the prevalent and steady principles of America. that you might destroy their towns, and cut them off from the superfluities, perhaps the conveniences of life, but that they were prepared to despise your power, and would not lament their loss, whilst they had—*what*, my Lords?—their woods and liberty. The name of my authority, if I am called upon, will authenticate the opinion irrefragably.

If illegal violences have been, as it is said, committed in America, prepare the way, open a door of possibility, for acknowledgment and satisfaction. But proceed not to such coercion, such proscription: cease your indiscriminate inflictions, amerce not thirty thousand, oppress not three millions, for the faults of forty or fifty. Such severity of injustice must forever render incurable the wounds you have already given your Colonies; you irritate them to unappeasable rancor. What though you march from town to town, and from province to province?

Though you should be able to force a temporary and local submission, which I only suppose, not admit, how shall you be able to secure the obedience of the country you leave behind you in your progress? To grasp the dominion of 1800 miles of continent, populous in valor, liberty, and resistance? This resistance to your arbitrary system of taxation might have been foreseen; it was obvious from the nature of things and of mankind; and above all, from the Whiggish spirit flourishing in that country. The spirit which now resists your taxation in America, is the same which formerly opposed, and with success opposed, loans, benevolences, and ship-money in England—the same spirit which called all England *on its legs*, and by the Bill of Rights vindicated the English Constitution—the same spirit which established the great fundamental and essential maxim of your liberties, that no subject shall be taxed, *but by his own consent*. If your Lordships will turn to the politics of those times, you will see the attempts of the Lords to poison this inestimable benefit of the Bill, by an insidious proviso: you will see their attempts defeated, in their conference with the Commons, by the decisive arguments of the ascertainers and maintainers of our liberty: you will see the thin, inconclusive, and fallacious stuff of those enemies to freedom, contrasted with the sound and solid reasoning of Serjeant Glanville and the rest, those great and learned men who adorned and enlightened this country, and placed her security on the summit of justice and freedom. And whilst I am on my legs, and thus do justice to the memory of those great men, I must also justify the merit of the living by declaring my firm and fixed opinion, that such a man exists this day, [looking towards Lord Camden].

This glorious spirit of Whiggism animates three millions in America, who prefer poverty with liberty, to golden chains and sordid affluence; and who will die in defence of their rights, as men—as freemen. What shall oppose this spirit, aided by the congenial flame glowing in the breast of every Whig in England, to the amount, I hope, of at least double the American numbers? Ireland they have to a man. In that country, joined as it is with the cause of the Colonies, and placed at their head, the distinction I contend for, is and must be observed. This country superintends and controls their trade and navigation; but they *tax themselves*. And this distinction between external and internal control, is sacred and insurmountable; it is involved in the abstract nature of things. Property is private, individual, absolute. Trade is an extended and complicated consideration; it reaches as far as ships can sail, or winds can blow. It is a great and various machine. To regulate the numberless movements of its several parts, and combine them into effect for the good of the whole, requires the superintending wisdom and energy of the supreme power in the empire. But this supreme power has no effect towards internal taxation, for it does not exist in that relation. There is no such thing, no such idea in this Constitution, as a supreme power operating upon property.

Let this distinction then remain forever ascertained. Taxation is theirs, commercial regulation is ours. As an American, I would recognize to England her supreme right of regulating commerce and navigation. As an Englishman by birth and principle, I recognize to the Americans their supreme unalienable right in their property; a right which they are justified in the defence of, to the last extremity. To maintain this principle is the common cause of the Whigs on the other side of the Atlantic, and on this. 'Tis liberty, to liberty engaged, that they will defend themselves, their families, and their country. In this great cause they are immovably allied. It is the alliance of God and nature—immutable, eternal, fixed as the firmament of heaven! To such united force, what force shall be opposed? *What*, my Lords; a few regiments in America, and seventeen or eighteen thousand men at home! The idea is too ridiculous to take up a moment of your Lordships' time; nor can such a national principled union be resisted by the tricks of office or ministerial manœuvres. Laying papers on your tables, or counting noses on a division, will not avert or postpone the hour of danger. It must arrive, my Lords, unless these fatal acts are done away; it must arrive in all its horrors: and then these boastful Ministers, 'spite of all their confidence and all their manœuvres, shall be forced to hide their heads. But it is not repealing this Act of Parliament, or that Act of Parliament,—it is not repealing a *piece* of *parchment* that can restore America to your bosom. You must repeal her fears and her resentments, and you may then hope for her love and gratitude. But now insulted with an armed force posted in Boston, irritated with an hostile array before her eyes, her concessions, if you could force them, would be suspicious and insecure: they will be *irato animo:* they will not be the sound, honorable pactions of freemen: they will be the dictates of fear and the extortions of force. But it is more than evident that you *cannot* force them, principled and united as they are, to your unworthy terms of submission. It is impossible. And when I hear General

Gage censured for inactivity, I must retort with indignation on those whose intemperate measures and improvident councils have betrayed him into his present situation. His situation reminds me, my Lords, of the answer of a French General in the civil wars of France, Monsieur Turenne, I think. The Queen said to him with some peevishness, "I observe that you were often very near the Prince during the campaign, why did you not take him ?" The Mareschal replied with great coolness, "J' avois grand peur, qui Monsieur le Prince ne me pris,"—I was very much afraid the Prince would take me.

When your Lordships look at the papers transmitted us from America, when you consider their decency, firmness, and wisdom, you cannot but respect their cause, and wish to make it your own. For myself I must declare and avow that in all my reading and observation, and it has been my favorite study—I have read Thucydides, and have studied and admired the master states of the world, —that for solidity and reasoning, force of sagacity, and wisdom of conclusion, under such a complication of different circumstances, no nation or body of men can stand in preference to the general Congress at Philadelphia. I trust it is obvious to your Lordships, that all attempts to impose servitude on such men, to establish despotism over such a mighty continental nation—must be vain—must be fatal. We shall be forced ultimately to retract, whilst we can, not when we must. I say we must necessarily undo these violent and oppressive acts :—they must be repealed—you will repeal them : I pledge myself for it you will in the end repeal them : I stake my reputation on it: I will consent to be taken for an idiot if they are not finally repealed. Avoid then this humiliating, disgraceful necessity. With a dignity becoming your exalted situation, make the first advances to concord, to peace and happiness, for that is your true dignity, to act with prudence and with justice. That you should first concede is obvious from sound and rational policy. Concession comes with better grace and more salutary effect from the superior power. It reconciles superiority of power with the feelings of men; and establishes solid confidence in the foundation of affection and gratitude. So thought the wisest poet and perhaps the wisest man in political sagacity, the friend of Mæcenas, and the eulogist of Augustus. To him, the adopted son and successor of the first Cæsar—to him, the master of the world, he wisely urged this conduct of prudence and dignity.

Tuque prior, &c. VIRGIL.

Every motive therefore of justice and of policy, of dignity and of prudence, urges you to allay the ferment in America, by a removal of your troops from Boston, by a repeal of your Acts of Parliament, and by demonstration of amicable dispositions towards your Colonies. On the other hand, every danger and every hazard impend to deter you from perseverance in your present ruinous measures: foreign war hanging over your heads by a slight and brittle thread: France and Spain watching your conduct, and waiting for the maturity of your errors; with a vigilant eye to America and the temper of your Colonies, more than to their own concerns, be they what they may.

To conclude, my Lords, if the Ministers thus persevere in misadvising and misleading the King, I will not say that they can alienate his subjects from his crown, but I will affirm that they will make the crown not worth his wearing : I shall not say that the King is betrayed, but I will pronounce *that the kingdom is undone*.

CPSIA information can be obtained
at www.ICGtesting.com
Printed in the USA
LVHW021926230822
726679LV00003B/435